TOM BROWN

The HEAVEN'S GATE

Suicide

Unlocking the answer to why it happened

The Heaven's Gate Suicide: Unlocking the answer to why it happened.

Cover designed by Gloria Williams-Méndez

Tom Brown
P.O. Box 27275
El Paso, TX 79926
(915) 855-9673
Email: tombrown@whc.net
Internet: www.tbm.org

ISBN: 0-9658305-0-0
Printed in the United States of America
Copyright 1997 by Tom Brown

Contents

Introduction

The Heaven's Gate Suicide

It could have happened anywhere. But the beautiful community of Rancho Santa Fe was not the likely place. The town is like the pocket where the Creator keeps all his prized possessions. Palm trees glisten along the winding, hilly roads leading to this gated community of million dollar mansions.

But at 18241 Colina Norte, an unseen, eerie, darkness was hovering over the estate. Unknown to the neighbors, Herff Applewhite, had brainwashed his thirty-eight followers to the point where they were willing to commit suicide in the hopes that they would be whisked away by a space ship that was supposed to be flying in the slipstream of the Hale-Bopp comet.

I first heard the tragic news when I arrived home from an evening prayer meeting. I turned on the television to see the interview with Larry King and Pastor Benny Hinn. Larry asked Pastor Benny, how God could have allowed this tragedy in San Diego to happen? That was the first I heard of this tragedy.

This question posed by Larry King is being asked by millions. Benny Hinn gave the answer that few Americans are willing to hear: "Demons caused these people to kill themselves." Larry was silent. I'm sure most Americans who were watching this interview were stunned by the pastor's answer. But he was right!

Sounds too simple? Well, the Bible provides simple answers. When I say "simple" I don't mean "simplistic." There is nothing simplistic about the devil and evil spirits. But they are real, nevertheless.

Demons Are Real

It is now time that Americans face the fact that the Bible is right. Demons are real, and they work to deceive people into doing the craziest things.

I realize that as humans, we can do some dumb things without the help of demons, but it takes something far greater than ourselves to make us commit suicide. Yes, humans are not so bright, but are humans so stupid as to "pack suitcases" when they're not going to need them if they shed their "container" bodies? Let's face it, no one on their own could contrive such a stupid act. The Bible explains that demons deceive humans to do such insane things.

The Bible Predicted This

The Bible foretells this tragedy and others like it:

> *The Spirit clearly says that in later times some will abandon the faith and follow deceiving spirits and things taught by demons. Such teachings come through hypocritical liars, whose consciences have been seared as with a hot iron. They forbid people to marry and order them to abstain from certain foods, which God created to be received with thanksgiving by those who believe and who know the truth. (1 Tim. 4:1-3)*

The cult leader Marshall Herff Applewhite was raised in a Christian home. His father was a Presbyterian minister. He even had aspirations to become a minister like his father. He, however, had problems with homosexuality. As a result, he left a teaching job at the University of Alabama in the '60s amid rumors of an affair with a male student.

This led to his eventual abandoning of Christianity. **Some will abandon the faith** the Bible says. He was unknowingly following **deceiving spirits and things taught by demons.** He combined Christian lingo with New Age teaching, Eastern religions, metaphysics, astrology, gnosticism, evolution, and a strong belief in UFO's. He practiced and taught his followers that marriage should be avoided, the very thing that the Bible warns that false teachers will do: **They forbid people to marry.**

The problem with this group is that they did not **believe and...know the truth.** When a person or group of persons do not accept the truth of the gospel as openly presented in the pages of the Bible, then deception can easily follow. The best protection from demonic lies is to know the Bible.

One of the misconceptions about the Heaven's Gate cult and cult leaders, such as Jim Jones and David Koresh, is that people think these people knew the Bible, and that's why they lost their minds. But the truth is, they did not know the Bible, or else, they could have distinguished between the truth in the Bible from the twisted lies of their leaders. The Bible even warns about these false leaders:

> *But there were also false prophets among the people, just as there will be false teachers among you. They will secretly introduce destructive heresies, even denying the sovereign Lord who bought them—bringing swift destruction on themselves. (2 Pet. 2:1)*

They teach destructive heresies because they are "ignorant and unstable people" who "distort" the "Scriptures" (2 Pet. 3:16). The devil distorted the Scriptures when he tempted Christ in the wilderness by trying to get Christ to kill Himself by throwing Himself off the pinnacle of the temple. But Christ simply rejected Satan's twisted logic by quoting the Word of God in its context. If Applewhite had known the real teaching of the Scriptures, he would have avoided this temptation of the devil as Christ had done.

The major problem with most Americans and, in fact the world, is that they know very little about the Bible. They are ripe for deception. There are thousands of cults across America. Expect for more people to enter cults, unless America returns back to its heritage of the Bible.

I realize that most people won't get involved in cults like Heaven's Gate, but they will live mixed up lives. They will not be able to stay married; instead they will divorce. They will get trapped by drugs and alcohol. They will feel depressed and miserable. All of these things are caused by deceiving spirits as well.

The Bible says that the devil "leads the whole world astray" (Rev. 12:9). Not only did the devil lead this cult astray, but he tries to lead everyone astray. The only protection from Satan's deception is to know the Word of God.

Do You Know the Bible?

Are you well versed in the Bible? Do you understand what it teaches about God, Jesus, the Holy Spirit, salvation, heaven, hell, demons, angels, miracles, tongues, etc.? The best thing you can do for you and your loved ones, is to get involved in an organized study of the Bible. And don't accept just one person's interpretation, but study the Bible for yourself. Then read what many others have to say about the Scriptures, especially those Christian leaders who are well respected in the Body of Christ. Don't live on just one person's interpretation.

In this book, I want to present to you a systematic study of the devil and demons. I'm not doing this so that you can concentrate on the devil, but so that you can understand his strategies. The Bible teaches that you are in a war against Satan (Ep 6:12). As a good soldier, you must prepare for war by conducting surveillance on the enemy. You don't do this because you want to fellowship with the foe, but so that you can understand the strengths, weaknesses, and strategies of your adversary.

What You Will Learn

This book will explain how demons got control over the Heaven's Gate cult and their leader, and, most importantly, this book will show you how they get control of people today. It will provide the Bible answer to this tragedy, and how to avoid it in the future. This book will take you through a solid study of the Bible, so you'll be able to identify Satan's strategies and how he works in people's lives.

What This Book Will Do For You

This book will not simply satisfy your curiosity about this cult, but it will help you see Satan working all around you.

You see, you don't need to wait for a tragedy like this to see Satan working. All you have to do is go to the nearest hospital, and you'll see the devil working at destroying innocent lives. Go to the court house, and you'll see the devil operating. Run to the nearest marriage counselor, and you'll see the devil working to destroy marriages. Take a stroll in the poorest neighborhood where hopes have been robbed, and you'll see Satan working.

Actually, you don't have to go anywhere to see Satan working, because he is working on you as well. The depression and fear you have felt is from him. The confusion you have experienced is from him. The lack of money in your account is from him. The illness in your body is from him.

Don't be frightened! The Bible provides the answer to the devil's power. You can have victory over him, and this book will show you how! But you have to begin by understanding that Satan is really behind the evil in this world.

THE HEAVEN'S GATE SUICIDE

Chapter 1

Why Bad Things Happen

Why did God allow it? Larry King's question to Pastor Benny Hinn shows that many people think that God should have stopped the mass suicide near San Diego from happening. The question further implies that somehow God must take some responsibility for this tragedy.

You see, this question hits to the heart of the matter which matters most to people, and that has to do with the question: Why do bad things happen? If God is in control, why does He permit bad things to happen?

The truth is, God has nothing to do with the bad things in our lives. The Bible clearly teaches that bad things happen because Satan causes them. The devil is the one who tries to bring bad things in our lives. It's important that you understand that Satan is the trouble maker.

God is good, and Satan is bad. That may sound elementary, but this is good theology. Don't be confused about the origin of tragedy. Satan is your enemy, and he brings bad and not good.

The Bullfighter

Next to my city of El Paso is Juarez, Mexico. One of the top sports there is bullfighting. You've seen how bullfighters put to death the bulls. They hold out a red cape in order to temp the bull to gore the phantom enemy. The bull sticks down its head, kicks up some sand, and heads angrily toward the cape, only to be surprised by a sword appearing out of nowhere.

During one match as the bullfighter had plunged several swords into the bull, a spectator could be heard saying, "If that bull ever finds out who's sticking him, then the bullfighter has had it!" The same is true of you. If you ever find out that it is the devil who's been sticking you, then the devil has had it.

The Tester

I once was playing Bible Trivia with a few guys, when the following question was asked: "Who put the Church of Smyrna in prison to test them?"

The guy answering, smiled real big and confidently answered, "God, of course!" Everyone nodded their heads as if he answered correctly.

I spoke up, "Wrong. The answer is the devil. He put them in prison to test them."

Everyone looked at me as if I was a heretic. I could almost hear their minds, "What!? Are you crazy? Don't you know that God is the One who tests us?" Someone pointed to the fellow holding the card and told him to read the answer.

The person turned over the card and slowly read it. You could see the shock on his face. "Tom's right. It says that the devil put them in prison."

"No, that couldn't be right!" everyone argued.

"The Bible Trivia is right," I defended. "Look up Revelation and you'll see that it was the devil, and not God, who put the church in prison." They looked it up:

> Do not be afraid of what you are about to suffer. I tell you, the devil will put some of you in prison to test you, and you will suffer persecution for ten days" (Revelation 2:10)

After reading this Scripture I was able to teach the guys the truth about test and trials.

The Truth About Test And Trials

There is not a passage of Scripture which I think addresses this issue about test and trials like James chapter one. This chapter clearly teaches that God is *not* the cause of trials.

> *When tempted, no one should say, "God is tempting me."*
> *For God cannot be tempted by evil, nor does he tempt anyone;*
> *(James 1:13)*

This makes it abundantly clear that God is not the author of temptations and trials. He's not the author of the tragedy in San Diego. Someone may argue, "There is a difference between a temptation and a trial. God doesn't tempt us, but He does send us trials." People who argue this point miss the Greek text.

The Greek word for **tempted** is *peirazo*. It is the same word used for "trials" and "trial" in verses 2 and 12 of that same chapter:

> *Consider it pure joy, my brothers, whenever you face trials*
> *of many kinds...*
> *Blessed is the man who perseveres under trial, because*
> *when he has stood the test, he will receive the crown of life*
> *that God has promised to those who love him.*

The point is simple: In the Hebrew mind there was no distinction between a temptation and a trial. They knew that both came from the enemy.

Today's theologian, in order to avoid the obvious, will try to make a distinction between a temptation (lust for money) and a trial (becoming sick), however in the Apostle James' understanding, he doesn't see the difference, and does not use a different Greek word for trial and temptation. We should not see any difference between the two, either.

As in the case of the Heaven's Gate suicide, the temptation to commit suicide led to tragedy. Was the suicide a temptation or a trial? It's both. It's ridiculous to try and distinguish whether this was a trial or a temptation. The point is, a great tragedy took place, and God had nothing to do with it.

James 1:16-17 definitely makes it clear that James has in mind both trials and temptations, because he writes:

Don't be deceived, my dear brothers. Every good and perfect gift is from above, coming down from the Father of the heavenly lights, who does not change like shifting shadows.

The fact that James warns the brothers about being deceived shows how easily it is to be deceived in this area. Many sincere believers are deceived into believing that the Father in heaven sends bad things our way, but this Scripture should end the debate about this issue. The Heaven's Gate cult saw suicide as a blessing instead of a curse. Satan deceived them by making them see bad things as good things.

In fact one family member of the cult, said that her brother "made his choices, and we respect those choices." She's wrong! We can not respect any choice that is made as a result of the devil's deception. Suicide is bad—pure and simple!

God Is Not A Killer

The doctrine that God causes tragedy is evil because it misrepresents the character of God. How would you like to be accused of killing someone? Well, this is what many have done. They have blamed God for the misery in this world, but He's not to be blamed.

This teaching that blames God for calamities and afflictions is also unhealthy, because it causes Christians to be passive and not actively fight off Satan's attacks. After all, if you think that God is the One Who wants you to kill yourself, then you will not fight off the temptation to commit suicide, in fact you will embrace it. This is exactly what Satan caused this cult to do. They embraced suicide as good, instead of fighting it as bad.

Fire Trucks Don't Start Fires

Some even think that this tragedy is a blessing in disguise. It was not a blessing. It was a tragedy.

Many people approach Satan's tragedies in their lives as blessings because they claimed to have learned so much from their tragedy. You hear people say, "I've learned so much from my trials. God was with me during my trials, and eventually delivered me. He must have been the One who caused it or allowed it so that I can learn."

This reminds me of a little boy who lived next to a fire station. Every time the fire truck left on a call, the little boy asked his dad, "Where's that truck going?"

The dad would answer every time, "The truck is going to a fire."

This kind of questioning went on for many days, until the boy in exasperation said, "Daddy, why doesn't somebody stop that truck from starting fires?"

People are like that little boy. God is always with us, rescuing us from our trials, so people assume God must be the One going around starting trials. But He's the One rescuing us from trials. "The Lord knows how to rescue godly men from trials" (2 Peter 2:9). God rescues us from trials; He doesn't cause them.

Weight Bar Bell

You might ask, "Don't trials make us strong?" Not by themselves. You see, there is an element of truth about trials strengthening us, but often people take this teaching to the extreme. It is not trials which strengthen us, but it is resisting those trials which strengthen us. This is what James meant for us to do—he wants us to resist our trials:

> ...*you know that the testing of your faith develops perseverance. Perseverance must finish its work so that you may be mature and complete, not lacking anything. (James 1:3-4)*

Perseverance does not mean putting up with the problem; it means to actively fight against the difficulties. Someone who perseveres resists the trials, and resisting them makes people strong. "Resist the devil, and he will flee from you" (James 4:8).

Let me illustrate it this way. A trial is like a weight barbell. Imagine you lying on your back with this weight on you. Do you become strong by allowing the weight to press down on you? No, you only become strong when you push the weight off of you.

This is true concerning trials. You don't become strong by allowing the trial to stay on you. You only become strong when you push the trial from you.

James says that perseverance will make you **mature and complete, not lacking anything**. Two wonderful results occur when you resist your trials: first, you will be mature and complete, that is you will become strong; second, you will not lack anything, which means that you will have overcome the trial.

God's Hired Hand

Many people have finally realized that the Bible attributes tragedy to Satan, nevertheless people still want to hold on to the view that God must still be responsible in some way for this tragedy. I went to a minister's conference in Florida. In particular I wanted to hear one of my favorite Bible teachers. Generally, he's a great teacher, but this time he took off on this confusing doctrine.

He said, "God is not the One causing problems; Satan is. However, Satan is God's hired hand."

I almost fell off my chair when I heard this outlandish assertion. According to him, "Satan is the hatched man. God has now become a Mafia Godfather, hiring Satan as his hit-man. God is too good to cause tragedy, so He hires Satan to do his dirty work." This still makes God an accomplice with Satan. How terrible to accuse God of joining in with Satan to cause trouble in people's lives.

For the next fifteen minutes this minister tried to convince us pastors that Satan is working under God's control, and that everything Satan does God permits him to do it. I got so tired of this, I simply left the room. Unfortunately, some people stayed to eat this poison. Later, these ministers were going back to their churches to feed this poison to their members. No wonder we have such confusion in the Church.

Does this preacher really think that God sent the devil to this cult to test them?

Listen to me carefully: God and Satan are archenemies. They have nothing in common. God works for the good of people; Satan works to cause bad things to happen. Satan does not work for God.

God has good angels that serve us. God's angels are ministering spirits sent to serve us, not to harm us (Heb. 1:14). Don't let anyone confuse you regarding this issue.

The Thief

Jesus said, "The thief cometh not, but for to steal, and to kill, and to destroy: I am come that they might have life, and that they might have it more abundantly" (John 10:10, KJV). This is the line of demarcation between Jesus and Satan. Jesus calls Satan a thief. A thief is interested in only one thing: to take what belongs to others. A thief is successful if he can steal secretly, and better yet, if he can frame someone else with the crime.

This is what Satan as a thief does. He steals secretly, so that people don't even know it was him who stole. And then he frames God with the crime. So people go around thinking that God is the One Who makes them sick, or causes them to lose their jobs, or destroy their marriages or makes people commit suicide.

Has Satan played this trick on you? Here you are going through a trial, and in your mind you are unsure who's to blame. Then this thought comes to you, "Maybe God is behind my trial. Perhaps He's using this to test me." Do you know what has happened to you? You have been deceived by Satan; he's planted evidence in your mind that God is the One guilty of causing your trial. Reject those thoughts. They are contrary to the Word of God.

Satan Causes Sickness

Jesus always saw Satan as the One who caused sickness or trouble. He rebuked storms, which shows that storms are not "acts of God." Jesus would minister to a sick person, and rebuke the spirit of infirmity. He saw sickness as evil spirits. He told the sick, "Be healed." He took for granted that it was always God's will to heal.

When dealing with a woman who was sick for many years, Jesus said, "Should not this woman, a daughter of Abraham, whom Satan has kept bound for eighteen long years, be set free...from what bound her?" (Luke 13:16). Jesus was convinced that Satan was the person who bound people with sickness. Are you just as convinced?

Jesus laid hands on Peter's mother in law. She was in bed with a fever. The Bible says, "So [Jesus] bent over her and rebuked the fever, and it left her" (Luke 4:39). He rebuked the fever. Jesus would never rebuke anything which might remotely be of God. He rebuked only things which were of Satan. This makes sickness of Satan.

Peter comments on Jesus' ministry of healing:

how God anointed Jesus of Nazareth with the Holy Spirit and power, andhow he went around doing good and healing all who were under the power of the devil, because God was with him. (Acts 10:38)

Peter knew the truth that the devil made people sick and was out to kill people, and Jesus came to deliver people from the devil's power. Have you grasped this truth as well? I hope so.

Once you are convinced that Satan is your enemy and that he's the one who opposes you with trouble, sickness, poverty, trials, and all that is bad, then you will boldly rebuke him and cast him out of your life. You'll be able to resist any temptation or trial that tries to rob you from the abundant life that Jesus came to give you.

The God Of The Old Testament

This leaves us with a question: Why does the Old Testament attribute tragedy (pestilence, calamities, etc.) to God? You don't have to read very much in the Old Testament to discover that it describes God as bringing sickness, poverty, disasters, and death to people. Many Christians scratch their heads, perplexed, wondering why God would do such horrible things.

The first thing you must realize is this: The Bible is a progressive revelation of God. The New Testament is the highest revelation of the heart of God. We, therefore, interpret those Old Testament passages about God causing tragedy in light of the New Testament—not the other way around. Since the New Testament makes it clear that the cause of tragedy is Satan, we must accept that, despite what we read from the Old Testament.

I find it disturbing that people will try to prove that God causes tragedy by referring to the Old Testament, instead of using the New Testament to prove this. They have to do this because they know that the New Testament makes it abundantly clear that God is the healer, and that the devil is the destroyer.

Does this mean that the Old Testament is wrong? No, the Old Testament is simply God's Word under construction. You can't tell what a building looks like by simply seeing the foundation; you must wait until it's finished before you can describe the whole building.

When we began to build our church facility, many of our members were concerned that the structure was too small. All they had to go by was the foundation that was laid. To them the foundation seemed too small. But as they witnessed the continued construction and progressively saw the church built, they soon realized that the building was big.

This is true of the Bible. If all you had to go on about God was the Old Testament, you would have an incomplete picture of God. You must read all of the Bible to get a complete picture of God. The Old Testament shows that God is a God of justice—He will punish those who disobey Him.

19

The New Testament shows that God's justice has been finally satisfied by the sacrifice of Jesus on the cross. The cross defeated Satan. So with Satan's defeat accomplished, God, through the New Testament, finally reveals the source of troubles as coming from Satan.

In the Old Testament, God allowed Israel to believe that He was the One bringing disasters on them for one main reason: to keep Israel from idolatry.

You see, God knew that Israel would pay homage to Satan if they found out that he was the one who brought sicknesses and calamities. All the other nations did this when they found out that there were many demons causing problems. These nations sacrificed to these demons which they called gods. Paul confirms this when he writes, "...the sacrifices of pagans are offered to demons, not to God" (1 Cor. 10:20).

God knew that Israel would do the same thing if they discovered that demons were responsible for sickness, poverty, and tragedy. So God took the blame for the calamities so that Israel would worship and sacrifice only to Him.

Occasionally, God allowed Israel to know that a fallen angel named Satan was responsible for illnesses, like the book of Job teaches. However, Israel never did see Satan as the enemy of God. They saw him simply as a messenger from God—one who was responsible to torment people under God's control. The Encyclopedia confirms this:

> In the Old Testament, Satan is not God's opponent. Instead, he searches out men's sins, and accuses mankind before God. [The World Book Encyclopedia, by Field Enterprises Educational Corporation, D Volume 5, 1976 page 141.]

God allowed Israel to think this because it would have been harmful for Israel to know that there was a rebellious angel who made people sick; because if they knew this, then Israel would have begun to sacrifice to him. It would have done no good for God to reveal to Israel that Satan was responsible for tragedy, because Israel could not have done anything about him since Satan had not yet been defeated. Israel would not be able to exercise authority over him. So if Israel could not defeat him, they would serve him. This would have been disastrous.

However, Jesus came and defeated the devil on the cross, and gave us His authority to overcome him. Since we have authority over Satan, God finally revealed the truth that Satan has always been in opposition to God. But now through the authority of Christ, we can oppose him successfully.

But under the Old Covenant, God's people did not have authority over Satan, so God allowed Israel to think that Satan was working for Him. Consequently, Israel kept their eyes only on God.

Today, though, we clearly understand that Satan is the enemy of God, and that he does not work for God in any capacity. It's good to know who the real enemy is, and that he is the source of troubles, since we now have authority over him and can stop his troubles.

THE HEAVEN'S GATE SUICIDE

Chapter 2

Who Deceived Them?

At this point, you may be wondering why God would even make the devil in the first place. After all, why would God make the devil if all he was going to do was cause tragedies and deceive people? That's a good question, and I will attempt to answer it now.

It is important that you understand what the Bible actually says about the original purpose of the devil. Unfortunately, the Heaven's Gate cult had a misconception about the devil.

This cult was obsessed with what they called the "Luciferians." This designation is based on the original name that the Bible gives to Satan. To them the Luciferians were "space alien races in opposition" to them. They believed that Luciferians were

> their ancestors [who] fell into disfavor with the Kingdom Level Above Human many thousands of years ago. They are not genderless—they still need to reproduce. They have become nothing more than technically advanced humans (clinging to human behavior) who retained some of what they learned while in the early training of Members of the Level Above Human, e.g., having limited: space-time travel, telepathic communication, advanced travel hardware (spacecrafts, etc.), increased longevity, advanced genetic engineering, and such skills as suspending holograms (as used in some so-called "religious miracles".) [parenthesis in the original]

This view about the devil and demons is totally in opposition to the Bible. It's important that you understand from the Bible who the devil really is, not what the Heaven's Gate cult thought he was.

The Bible tells us that the devil was originally created by God to be the most intelligent, beautiful archangel which God had ever made. God entrusted him by making him the chief executive of all the angels. His job was to stretched forth his wings in order to cover and guard God's throne. He was God's own sentinel. He was so important that he led the worship in heaven. His beauty lifted him in pride, however, and as a result he convinced one-third of the angels to make war against God in the hope that he could take over God's throne. He along with the rebellious angels were cast out of heaven. They now make war against us.

Where in the Bible does it mention all of these things about the devil? We find all these things in the Bible by beginning with the clear references about the devil, and from them, we can understand the equivocal references about him.

War in Heaven

And there was war in heaven. Michael and his angels fought against the dragon, and the dragon and his angels fought back. But he was not strong enough, and they lost their place in heaven. The great dragon was hurled down— that ancient serpent called the devil, or Satan, who leads the whole world astray. He was hurled to the earth, and his angels with him. (Revelation 12:7-9)

This clearly shows that the devil and his angels are not aliens flying in space crafts, but they are spiritual beings who operate on this earth. They are not "technically advanced humans."

A major error in this cult involved their belief that some humans were demons. To them, people were their enemies. The Bible makes it clear that we are not fighting with humans.

> *For we are not fighting against people made of flesh and*
> *blood, but against persons without bodies—the evil rulers of*
> *the unseen world, those mighty satanic beings and great evil*
> *princes of darkness who rule this world; and against huge*
> *numbers of wicked spirits in the spirit world. (Ep. 6:12,*
> *Living Bible)*

The Book of Revelation makes it clear that Satan once had a favorable position in heaven, but he was cast out of heaven and hurled to the earth. God did not make the devil to test us. He was not made for that original purpose.

The Scripture in Revelation gives us some keys to understanding a couple of Scriptures in the Old Testament, which deals with the fall of Satan. Those two passages are in Ezekiel chapter twenty-eight and Isaiah chapter fourteen.

The Garden of Eden

Let's look first at the Ezekiel passage. The Scripture in Revelation lets us know that Satan was **the ancient serpent** in the garden of Eden. Because of that, we know that Ezekiel chapter 28 deals with Satan:

> *The word of the Lord came to me: "Son of man, take up*
> *a lament concerning the king of Tyre and say to him: 'This*
> *is what the Sovereign Lord says: " You were the model of*
> *perfection, full of wisdom and perfect in beauty, You were in*
> *Eden, the garden of God... (Ez. 28:11-13)*

Other than God we know that there were only three beings in the garden of Eden: Adam, Eve, and the serpent. Ezekiel obviously could not be referring to the physical king of Tyre, because the king was not in the garden of Eden. After God expelled Adam and Eve from the garden, God sent angels to keep anyone from entering Eden. "After [God] drove the man out, he placed on the east side of the Garden of Eden cherubim and a flaming sword flashing back and forth to guard the way to the tree of life" (Genesis 3:24).

So the king of Tyre must be the ruling spirit over Tyre who happened to be Satan. Satan still rules kings, presidents, governors, mayors, political leaders, and even religious leaders if they let him. He tries to rule leaders, because by ruling leaders he can rule the world.

Satan works on religious leaders because if he can deceive them, he can ruin many lives. Charles Manson, Jim Jones, David Koresh, and recently, Herff Applewhite are examples of Satan deceiving religious leaders in order to destroy the lives of many people.

This is why God commands us to pray "for kings and all those in authority" (1 Timothy 2:2). God knows that leaders are Satan's top targets. We can accomplish more by praying for our leaders than by griping about them.

The great tragedy of the Heaven's Gate suicide is the fact that some people who knew them showed no real concerned about their spiritual lives. It's time that we become active in praying for people involved in cults, and especially praying for the false leaders so they can see the light. Then we must follow up our prayers by actively sharing the power of the gospel with them.

Model of Perfection

The passage in Ezekiel says, **You were a model of perfection**. God does not create anything which is imperfect. Don't think for a moment that God created the devil to be evil. God created him to be perfect.

God even says that he was **full of wisdom**. Satan was incredibly intelligent. He was smart. He still is a genius. There is something to note about his wisdom, though.

...you corrupted your wisdom... (Ez. 28:17)

Satan still has wisdom, but it is corrupted. James 3:15 says, "Such 'wisdom' does not come down from heaven but is earthly, unspiritual, of the devil." Do not underestimate Satan's ability to fool you. He is still a genius when it comes to deception.

People wonder, how can these thirty-nine educated people be fooled into committing suicide in the hope of being snatched into a flying saucer? The answer: Satan used his corrupted wisdom to deceive them.

The Bible also mentions how beautiful he was. He was **perfect in beauty**. Satan still uses his beauty to cause people to look upon him and his temptations as something desirable. He even "masquerades as an angel of light" (2 Corinthians 11:14). This means that he makes false teaching and lies seem like the truth. So he combines his corrupted wisdom with his beauty to deceive people.

This is what he did with this cult. He used Scriptures and twisted their meanings, then he combined the errors of various religions and philosophies to make his teaching appear attractive. The cult was eventually attracted to death! Satan is a great deceiver.

He is so good at it that the Bible says that he "leads the whole world astray" (Revelation 12:9). There is an old saying: You can fool some of the people all of the time, all of the people some of the time, but you can't fool all of the people all of the time. This saying is not true about Satan. He has fooled all the people of the earth. No one can claim that they haven't been fooled by him. He is a genius at deception.

He deceived the original couple, Adam and Eve. They were in a perfect environment, yet they sinned because Satan tempted them. One of the fallacies that people hold about those in cults is that they are raised in dysfunctional families. But as the evidence suggests in the Heaven's Gate cult, many of the people, including the leader, were raised in good homes.

The only way to counteract Satan's deceptions is to be filled with God's wisdom. No amount of intellectual knowledge will protect someone from deception. God's Word is the only protection. The wisdom of God is still wiser than Satan's wisdom. However, human wisdom is no match for Satan. He'll win the battle against anyone who depends on human wisdom.

Angel

Ezekiel goes on to say:

You were in Eden, the garden of God; every precious stone adorned you: ruby, topaz and emerald, chrysolite, onyx and jasper, sapphire, turquoise and beryl. Your settings and mountings were made of gold; on the day you were created they were prepared. You were anointed as a guardian cherub, for so I ordained you... (verses 13-14)

Satan was a cherub. A cherub is one of the classes of angels.

An angel is a ministering spirit. A spirit is unseen to the natural eyes. Just because people can't see Satan does not mean that he does not exist. He is just as real as good angels.

The Bible makes it clear that this rebellious angel was cast out of heaven and hurled to the earth. Not only was Satan cast out of heaven, but according to Revelation chapter 12:4 one-third of the angels fell with him:

His tail swept a third of the stars out of the sky and flung them to the earth.

Revelation continues,

And there was war in heaven. Michael and his angels fought against the dragon, and the dragon and his angels fought back. (verse 7)

The subject of angels is very popular today. Many books have been written about them. Yet, few people recognize the reality of evil angels. Most people think that all angels are good. But this is not true.

I find it disturbing that, with all the emphasis on angels in our day, very few people mention that one-third of the angels in the world are bad—they are against God and people. People are being tricked by bad angels. Many of the angel stories I've heard and read are unscriptural. You need to beware of evil angels, and not just aware of good angels.

Praise Leader

Not only was Satan an angel, but the Bible describes him as a **cherub**. According to the Bible, cherubim are around the throne of God giving praise and honor to God. Their main job is to praise God. This once was Satan's job. He used to praise God.

In fact according to the King James translation of Ezekiel 28:13, he has musical instruments built into him:

> *...the workmanship of thy tabrets and of thy pipes was prepared in thee in the day that thou wast created.*

He was a walking instrument of praise. This was his main purpose of creation; he was ordained for that purpose.

Just as Satan uses his wisdom and beauty to corrupt people, he uses his musical talent to corrupt them as well. He uses all kinds of music to entice peoples' passions. Music is used to promote sexual impurity; it is used to glorify drugs; it is used to sanction rebellion; it is used to endorse all kinds of sinful behavior. Satan is behind much of the music in the world today. You'll also find that music often plays an important part in a cult.

Guarding Angel

The Bible not only describes Satan as a cherub, but also as a **guardian** cherub. A guardian is one who protects, one who stands at the gate. This means that he was the angel that stood between God and rest of the angels. He was God's confidant. This powerful position was too much for this ego sensitive creature.

> *...So I drove you in disgrace from the mount of God, and expelled you, O guardian cherub, from among the fiery stones. Your heart became proud on account of your beauty, and you corrupted your wisdom, because of your splendor. So I threw you to the earth... (Ez. 28:16-17)*

The Apostle Paul gave instruction that no new convert should be a pastor, or else "he may become conceited and fall under the same judgment as the devil" (1 Timothy 3:6). This is what happened to Applewhite. He declared,

> I am in the same position to today's society as was the One that was in Jesus then. My being here now is actually a continuation of that last task as was promised, to those who were students 2000 years ago.

Applewhite was on an ego trip. Jesus warned us about people like Applewhite:

> *Jesus answered: "Watch out that no one deceives you. For many will come in my name, claiming, 'I am the Christ,' and will deceive many. (Matt. 24:4-5)*

Jesus says that **many will come in my name**. Look at history: It is filled with people using Jesus' name to claim that they are equal to Him. No one is equal to Christ. Christ stands alone as the only Savior of the world. As 1 Timothy 2:5 puts it: "For there is one God and one mediator between God and men, the man Christ Jesus."

Whenever someone puts a person between himself and God, then deception awaits. Don't put anyone as your mediator. Christ is the only mediator between God and people.

His Replacements

After Satan was expelled from heaven, God ordained two new angels to take over the position which Satan had.

> *And make two cherubim out of hammered gold at the ends of the cover. Make one cherub on one end and the second cherub on the other; make the cherubim of one piece with the cover, at the two ends. The cherubim are to have their*

wings spread upward, overshadowing the cover with them.
The cherubim are to face each other, looking toward the cover.
(Exodus 25:18-20)

In this passage we see clearly that there are two cherubim guarding the Ark of the Covenant, not just one cherub. The next time a cherub thinks he is so beautiful and that there is no one like him, all he has to do is look across and he'll see an exact copy of himself—that ends pride.

I believe Satan was the only cherub who guarded the throne of God. Now two cherubim have taken his place. They can never become prideful like Satan became, because they are not unique in beauty. I believe Satan was unique in beauty, this is why he was lifted up in pride.

I believe the lesson we can learn is to make sure that there is a plurality of leaders who are accountable to each other, instead of one man calling all the shots.

The early church was led by twelve apostles, not just one. Of course, Peter was the main leader, but even then, he was accountable to other men for his teachings and actions. Although Peter was the clear leader of the early church, he was still opened for correction as was in the case when the Apostle Paul rebuked him for showing favoritism (see Gal. 2:11-21).

A cult leader does not want to share his position of authority with anyone. Whenever you see a leader who listens to no one, then pray that he will humble himself. And in the meantime, help others get free from his dictatorial leadership.

High Ranking Angel

How great was this guardian cherub? Well, he was so great that one-third of the angels followed him in his rebellion. That's a lot of angels to rebel against God.

I believe that Satan must have been one of the top three angels in heaven, perhaps the highest angel. It could be rightly said that he was one of the archangels in heaven

Satan was not a Mickey mouse angel. He was no pipsqueak. He's not on the bottom wrung of the ladder. He was

31

one of the original archangels. It's important to understand this because one of the mistakes you can make in opposing him is to underestimate his power.

One of the cardinal mistakes in athletics is to underestimate your opponent. When a team begins to degrade their opponent before the game, then you can be sure that they will be in for a big surprise. A smart team never takes lightly their opponent. Even if they are much better than their opponent, they still show respect for them. When they do this, they are more likely to avoid obvious mistakes.

This is the mistake that friends and relatives made about this cult. They saw them as harmless, nice people who were involved in a different, though, benevolent religion. Don't underestimate what cults can do.

The Bible says that Satan "prowls around like a roaring lion looking for someone to devour" (1 Peter 5:8).

I think if I was out in the jungle and saw a lion who was observing me I would be concerned. And if he then booms out a ear-pitching roar, I would take him seriously. You, too, should take Satan seriously!

Lucifer's Fall from Grace

We now turn our attention to the passage in Isaiah chapter fourteen. Satan's original name is mentioned in Isaiah 14:12 (KJV):

> *How art thou fallen from heaven, O lucifer, son of the morning...*

It is from this passage that the Heaven's Gate cult came up with the term Luciferians. According to this cult some Luciferians are flying in spaceships, but according to this Scripture, Lucifer has fallen from heaven.

Jesus says, "I saw Satan fall like lightening from heaven" (Luke 10:18). From Jesus statement, we know that the passage in Isaiah is a clear reference to Satan.

He was called Lucifer. This name means morning star. This is a beautiful name, but Satan is no longer worthy of being called Lucifer. Don't ever address him as such. The only ones who address Satan as Lucifer are Satanists and cultists, such as Heaven's Gate. This shows how deceived they are.

Satan's Pride

All your pomp has been brought down to the grave, along with the noise of your harps... (Is. 14:11)

Again, here is another reference to Satan's musical ability and his being fired from his position of praise leader in heaven.

You said in your heart, "I will ascend to heaven; I will raise my throne above the stars of God; I will sit enthroned on the mount of assembly, on the utmost heights of the sacred mountain. I will ascend above the tops of the clouds; I will make myself like the Most High." But you are brought down to the grave, to the depths of the pit. (Is. 14:12-15)

Notice Satan's pride. He simply said over and over again, "**I will. I will. I will.**" Whenever you start talking like that then you too are in trouble.

"I will do as I please. I will do want I want to do. I will be the captain of my soul. I will be in charge of my life." This kind of talk is pride. You'll fall just like Satan fell.

Original Sin is Pride

Pride is the original sin of the universe. The original sin was not committed in Eden, but was committed in heaven. Satan fell into pride. Pride originate with Satan. Pride, therefore, is Satan's territory.

Whenever a person enters pride, he trespasses into Satan's region. This gives Satan permission to attack anyone in his territory. If you trespassed into someone's house, then they have a right to defend their home. They have a right to even shoot you, because you are a trespasser. The same is true of the devil.

This is why Satan had permission to destroy this cult. They were prideful. They believed that they alone were the representatives of God. Satan was able to destroy them because of pride.

> ... *"God opposes the proud but gives grace to the humble."*
> *Submit yourselves, then, to God. Resist the devil, and he will*
> *flee from you. (James 4:6)*

God is for us (Rom. 8:31). However, He can not be for those who are prideful. **God opposes the proud**. The only time God opposes anyone is when they are prideful.

Your ability to resist the devil is contingent on you humbling and submitting yourself to God. When you are truly humble and submissive to God, then you have the power to resist the devil, and he will flee from you.

Pride is the number one downfall of the greatest people in the world. Pride will bring down the most anointed minister, it will knock down the top athlete, it will smash the highest politician, it will shatter the most famous movie star, it will destroy the wealthiest entrepreneur. No prideful person escapes from the devil. The Heaven's Gate cult was no exception.

Chapter 3

Applewhite's Battle with Homosexuality

Shame led Herff Applewhite to check into a hospital, asking to be cured of his homosexual desires. Instead of submitting himself to the cross, where he could have been cleansed from guilt and sin, he allowed the accuser of the brothers to torment his soul with guilt. This eventually led him to castrate himself and lead an austere life, hoping to cleanse himself from guilt.

Today, many people do the same. For sure, most don't castrate themselves, but instead of accepting the cleansing power of the blood of Christ, they punish themselves by refusing to enjoy life. They believe they are too sinful to have nice things like a happy family and money to do fun things. The Heavens Gate cult looked down on Christian teaching that "promote[s] enriching their human lives and having them seek a 'Heaven on Earth.'"

Why were they against enjoying life when the Bible says that "God...richly provides us with everything for our enjoyment" (1 Tim. 6:17)? The answer is simple and is true of us as well: When you feel unworthy, you are unable to accept blessings from God. The devil will keep you from enjoying life by blaming you for your weaknesses. That's what the devil did to them.

You see, next to the name "Satan" the most prevalent name that the Bible gives him is "devil." It is used thirty-five times in the New Testament, and none in the Old Testament.

The name devil means accuser. Since this is the number two name which the Bible attributes to the fallen angel once named by God as Lucifer, then it stands to reason that his number two scheme against the believer is to make him feel guilty. Shame is a powerful weapon of Satan.

> ...*For the accuser of our brothers, who accuses them before our God day and night, has been hurled down. They overcame him by the blood of the Lamb and by the word of their testimony... (Rev 12:10-11)*

Second only to Satan's work in causing trials is the devil's work in causing guilt. These are his two main operations. The good news is that God has given us Someone greater than the devil so that we can overcome shame. He is the Holy Spirit. Unfortunately, many Christians, instead of seeing the Holy Spirit as the person Who help us overcome our guilt, see Him as the One who is responsible for our guilt.

For example, you hear many Christians say, "The Holy Spirit has convicted me of this sin." Wait a minute. Who's the guilt-maker: God or Satan?

The Conviction of the Holy Spirit

You say, "The Bible says that the Holy Spirit will convict us of sin." Well, let's see what the Bible actually says about the conviction of the Holy Spirit. It would do us good to see the work of the Holy Spirit as contrasted with the work of the devil when it comes to guilt.

The only place in the New Testament which mentions that the Holy Spirit convicts of sin is in John 16:7-8:

> ...*Unless I go away, the Counselor will not come to you; but if I go, I will send him to you. When he comes, he will convict the world of guilt in regard to sin...in regard to sin, because men do not believe in me;*

Who will the Holy Spirit convict? Jesus said that He will convict **the world**. Jesus did not say that He will convict the children of God. If Jesus believed that the Holy Spirit would convict the children of God, then why doesn't He mention it here? The fact that He does not mentioned this, shows clearly that the Holy Spirit was never meant to convict God's children.

The Holy Spirit convicts the world of sin. And why does the Holy Spirit convict the world? He convicts the world **"Because men do not believe in me."**

Let me ask you two questions: Do you belong to the world? No. And do you believe in Jesus? Yes. If you answered in this way, then the Holy Spirit does not convict you of guilt. The Holy Spirit convicts only those who belong to the world because they have rejected Christ.

Confession is Good for the Soul

The Holy Spirit is not the One who convicts you of guilt. He's not your prosecutor. Jesus called the Holy Spirit **the Counselor**. The Greek word for Counselor is *parakletos*. It is the normal word for defense attorney. This is where we get our English word "paralegal." A paralegal is a lawyer who stands next to his client in order to defend his innocence.

You see, the Holy Spirit is on your side. He's your defense attorney. His job is to protect you from being convicted. Yet many believers treat the Holy Spirit as though He was their prosecutor.

What would you do if you hired an attorney to represent you, and he told you that his goal was to convict you? You would quickly find another attorney. Yet, many Christians think that this is the reason God gave us the Holy Spirit. They think that God sent the Holy Spirit to convict us. If that's true, then the Holy Spirit makes a lousy attorney.

The goal of a defense attorney is to find you not guilty. This is what the Holy Spirit does. He finds you not guilty. He does not make you feel guilty. If you'll let Him lead you, He will remove the guilt from you. He will do this by leading you to confess your sin to God in order to be forgiven. "If we confess our sins, he is faithful and just and will forgive us our sins and purify us from all unrighteousness" (1 John 1:9).

God's solution for guilt is confession. Plead guilty, and

you'll be forgiven. The devil, though, will try to convince you that your sin is too great to be forgiven. Or he'll try to persuade you to deny that you've sinned. He may even tell you that what you did really was not sin. However, if the Word of God says it is sin, then it is sin. Confess it, and God will set you free from guilt.

"I have already confessed my sin a hundred times, but I still feel guilty. What's my problem?"

The trouble with you is that you've confessed your sin ninety-nine times too much. Simply confess in sincerity that you have sinned, and God promises to forgive you. Period! Now accept your forgiveness and go on with God.

Of course the problem with Applewhite was that he thought he was without sin. This of course led to further deception.

Conscience

"Well, if the Holy Spirit is not convicting me of sin, then why do I feel guilty when I sin?" You feel guilty because of your conscience.

The Bible says, "Dear friends, if our hearts do not condemn us, we have confidence before God" (1 John 3:21). It is our heart which convicts us when we do wrong. And it should, because this shows that we are truly saved. Our conscience is what hurts us when we sin.

However, don't confuse your conscience with the work of the Holy Spirit. The Holy Spirit does not need to convict the child of God, because He knows our conscience will convict us.

Quit saying, "The Holy Spirit has convicted me of this sin." Instead, say, "My heart has convicted me of this sin."

I've heard people try to make a distinction between "conviction" and "condemnation." They'll say, "The Holy Spirit does not condemn us but He does convict us." However, the word conviction means the same as condemnation. To convict means to find guilty in order to proceed with punishment. A court room uses the word conviction to describe someone who is found guilty. In fact, someone who's found guilty is called a convict.

The Holy Spirit has absolutely nothing to do with making you feel guilty as a Christian. When you understand this, you will be set free. No longer will you be wondering whether the Holy Spirit is convicting you or whether the devil is condemning you. If you've confessed your sin to God, then God has forgiven you. If you still feel guilty, then realize that the devil is accusing you of your past sin.

Don't think for a moment that the Holy Spirit is convicting you. Because He's not! It is the devil who is up to his old tricks. He's not called the devil for nothing. Devil means accuser.

Grieving the Spirit

"All right, maybe it's incorrect and not scriptural to say that the Holy Spirit convicts me, but it is scriptural to say that I've grieved the Holy Spirit."

I wonder what people mean when they say that they've "grieved the Holy Spirit." Usually they mean that they feel bad about something they've done. Again, they are back to attributing their feelings of guilt to the Holy Spirit. Only in this case, they use another term, "I've grieved the Holy Spirit."

And do not grieve the Holy Spirit of God, with whom you were sealed for the day of redemption. (Eph. 4:30)

From this Scripture people say with tears and pain, "I've grieved the Holy Spirit. I've sinned against Him." Okay, fine! So you've grieved the Holy Spirit. Then why are you hurt? After all, it's not you that are grieved; it's Him. Do you see what I mean?

If I walked up to you and slapped you on the cheek, who would feel the pain? Obviously, you would, because you were the one who was slapped. I would not be holding my cheek in pain claiming I've slapped you. It's not my cheek that hurts, it's yours.

Yes, it's possible to grieve the Holy Spirit. But remember, it is Him that's grieved, not you. It's Him that's hurt, not you.

THE HEAVEN'S GATE SUICIDE

I'll tell you the truth about it: if you've sinned and felt bad then you definitely have not grieved the Holy Spirit. He can only be grieved if you don't see your sin. If He sees that you feel sorry for what you've done, then He's happy that you see the error of your ways.

The danger in grieving the Holy Spirit is that you are unaware that you have grieved Him. This is serious sin.

This is one sin that helped destroy the Heaven's Gate cult. They honestly did not believe that they were sinning when they belittled the role Christ has in saving the world.

They mocked Christians who "say that God was incarnate as Jesus." Do you see what they did? They put down the deity of Jesus Christ. They refused to acknowledge that Jesus was God in human flesh. This sin totally grieved the Holy Spirit.

This sin caused the people to grow cold in their faith and love for Christ. It caused them to be ripe for deception as well.

I've brought all this up to show that guilt is not caused by the Holy Spirit, but by our conscience. If we have no conscience then we are liable to grieve the Holy Spirit. This was the problem with Applewhite. He was able to teach blasphemous doctrine because he was one of the false teachers that the Bible describes as one "whose consciences have been seared as with a hot iron" (1 Tim. 4:2).

Keep a sensitive conscience by acknowledging your sin, but don't go over board by condemning yourself.

The Weapon of Guilt

The devil uses our ignorance about forgiveness to bring needless guilt. Condemnation is such a powerful weapon against the believer, because condemnation robs the believer of every essential weapon that protects him from the devil. Ephesians 6:13-17 says,

> *Therefore put on the full armor of God, so that when the day of evil comes, you may be able to stand your ground, and after you have done everything, to stand. Stand firm then,*

*with the belt of truth buckled around your waist, with the
breastplate of righteousness in place, and with your feet fit-
ted with the readiness that comes from the gospel of peace. In
addition to all this, take up the shield of faith, with which
you can extinguish all the flaming arrows of the evil one.
Take the helmet of salvation and the sword of the Spirit,
which is the word of God.*

This is the classic Scripture about spiritual warfare. Paul
uses the battle armor of the Roman soldiers as an analogy of the
armor of believers. The two most important defensive pieces of
the armor are the breastplate and the helmet, because the most
fatal injuries occur in the heart and head. You can survive with
an injured toe or fight without a belt. But you can't survive if
your heart or head is injured.

Applewhite's mind was fatally injured because he did
not know how to appropriate the blood of Christ for forgiveness
of sins.

Notice that Paul places righteousness as the breastplate
that protects the heart and he places salvation as the helmet
which protects the head. Both righteousness and salvation protect against condemnation. When a person is under condemnation, then he has lost his sense of righteousness and hope
that he will be saved. Like Applewhite, he looks for another way
to be saved.

The Accuser

The Old Testament may not have used the name devil
to refer to Satan, but there is a clear reference to the accuser
working in the Old Testament.

*Then [the angel] showed me Joshua the high priest stand-
ing before the angel of the LORD, and Satan standing at his
right side to accuse him. The LORD said to Satan, "The
LORD rebuke you, Satan! The LORD, who has chosen
Jerusalem, rebuke you! Is not this man a burning stick
snatched from the fire?" Now Joshua was dressed in filthy*

clothes as he stood before the angel. The angel said to those who were standing before him, "Take off his filthy clothes." Then he said to Joshua, "See, I have taken away your sin, and I will put rich garments on you." (Zech. 3:1-4)

The way God removed Satan's ability to accuse Joshua was by removing his sin. Sin is the bases of Satan accusing us. Without sin, he has nothing to accuse us before God. God has removed our sin, thus, He removed Satan's means of accusing us.

God's answer for guilt is in the redemption of Christ. Through the cross, Jesus took away our sin, and put on us His **rich garments** of righteousness. Righteousness is the ability to stand before God without a sense of guilt, fear, or inferiority. This brings us logically to the redemption of the cross, and how it relates to Satan's defeat.

Chapter 4

The Devil Won

Satan is a worthy adversary, but he is defeated as far as the believer is concerned. Unfortunately, the Heaven's Gate cult lost the battle with Satan. The devil won!

But for true believers, Jesus has already won the battle, and He simply calls upon them to occupy until He comes. Jesus said, "Occupy till I come" (Luke 19:13, KJV). The word "occupy" is a military term. You have heard of an occupational force, haven't you? This is what we are: an occupational force.

An occupational force is sent in only when the war is won. The force then simply occupies by stopping any pockets of resistance that may still lurk in the region. This is what we do.

We remind the devil that Jesus won the battle, that he is defeated and has no authority over the Church. Then we take the weapons which God has given us and use them to stop him. We are not even worried about the outcome, because we know that we are in charge—not him. Christ's victory is our victory.

So our battle with the devil resembles more a gorilla war, where you have rebels who refuse to acknowledge the right of the legitimate government to rule. Jesus Christ is the rightful ruler of the world, and Satan and his cohorts are the rebels who try to fight the Lord Jesus and His army—but they will not overrule God's government!

You Can Relish Life

The Applewhite cult, however, did not see Satan as defeated. They believed that Satan was the winner—this is why they escaped from this earth. They believed that Satan was more powerful than them. To them, the world was doomed because Satan was in charge.

When you understand that Satan is defeated, then you can relish life. Life becomes wonderful, because you have the victory over the devil. You don't look for an escape from this earth.

You don't have to look at the Heaven's Gate cult to find people wanting to escape life; people are wanting to die all the time. Many go through with it, others are too frighten to do it. For some, life has become too difficult and painful to keep on living.

This may be you. But friend, Satan is defeated, and no matter what he tries to bring your way, you can overcome.

Jesus Triumphant

You may wonder how Christ defeated the devil for us. Jesus defeated the devil for us in three ways: through His earthly ministry, through His substitution, and through the new creation.

First, He defeated Satan through His earthly ministry. While Jesus was on earth, He successfully resisted the devil's temptations. He also cast out demons wherever they were. Demons cried out in fear whenever they saw Jesus. Often they cried, "Jesus, Son of David, why have you come to torment us before our time." Jesus simply drove them out of people.

The Substitution

Second, Jesus defeated the devil through His Substitutionary sacrifice on the cross:

When you were dead in your sins and in the uncircumcision of your sinful nature, God made you alive with Christ. He forgave us all our sins, having canceled the written code, with its regulations, that stood opposed to us; he took it

away, nailing it to the cross. And having disarmed the pow-
ers and authorities, he made a public spectacle of them, tri-
umphing over them by the cross. (Col. 2:13-15)

Jesus triumphed! He triumphed over the devil! And He did it
for you.

Jesus stripped Satan of his authority over mankind. He
needed to do this because the first man, Adam, handed over his
authority to Satan. God gave Adam dominion over the whole
earth (Genesis 1:26). Adam was in charge, but when he dis-
obeyed God by listening to the devil, he unknowingly obeyed
the serpent. By obeying him, Adam became a slave of Satan.
"You are slaves to the one you obey" (Romans 6:16).

So when Adam sinned he lost his authority and dominion over the world; and, instead, Satan took it. We know Satan
had the authority because when he tempted Christ in the
wilderness, he said, "I will give you all their authority and splen-
dor, for it has been given to me, and I can give it to anyone I
want to" (Luke 4:6). Jesus did not dispute Satan's claim to
authority, but instead He simply resisted the temptation to worship Satan.

Someone might argue, "Satan lied to Jesus. He boasted
of something that he did not have. He tried to trick Jesus."

If that was true, then Jesus was deceived. But He was not
deceived. And if Satan really did not have the authority which
he claimed, then Jesus was not really tempted. Because a
bonafide temptation must be legitimate; therefore, Satan must
have had the authority he claimed.

For example, if a poor man without a dime promised
you a million dollars if you would commit a crime for him, you
would easily shrug off his offer, because you know that he can't
make it good. You are not even tempted with his offer. However,
if a multimillionaire made the same offer, you might be tempted because you know that he has the money to pay you.

So if Satan did not have the kingdoms of the world then
Jesus would not have been tempted. This illustrates the fact that
Satan had the authority over the world.

Eat the Dust

Right after the Fall God asked Eve what she had done. She told God that the serpent had deceived her. So God speaks to the serpent. In God's words to the serpent, He hints to the fact that Satan would be in charge.

He speaks to the serpent, who we know from Revelation 12:9, is the devil. He is called in that passage "the ancient serpent." He tells the serpent,

"Cursed are you above all the livestock and all the wild animals! You will crawl on your belly and you will eat dust all the days of your life. (Genesis 3:14)

At first glance, it appears that God is humbling the serpent by making him crawl on his belly. But a closer look at the entire chapter reveals something else. Remember the purpose for him to crawl on his belly was to **eat dust**. Now physical snakes do not eat dust. God is speaking of something else, something deeply spiritual. Let me explain.

Later in this chapter God speaks to Adam and says,

"Cursed is the ground because of you; through painful toil you will eat of it all the days of your life. It will produce thorns and thistles for you, and you will eat the plants of the field. By the sweat of your brow you will eat your food until you return to the ground, since from it you were taken; for dust you are and dust you will return." (vs. 17-19)

Notice that God calls Adam **dust**. Before the Fall, Adam is called a "living soul" (Genesis 2:7, KJV). After the Fall, he is called dust. What a difference!

Adam is **dust**; the serpent is told to **eat dust**. Do you see the connection? The serpent was to feed on Adam's carnal nature. You've heard the phrase, "I am going to eat your lunch." This phrase means that "I am going to defeat you."

God is saying to the serpent, "You are going to eat Adam's lunch. You are going to defeat him." God was already declaring Satan's supremacy over Adam and his descendants. Satan would be in charge of the Adamic race.

However, concerning the war over the woman and her offspring, God said to the serpent,

> *"And I will put enmity between you and the woman, and between your offspring and hers; he will crush your head, and you will strike his heel." (v. 15)*

God declares that her offspring, or literally, "the seed of the woman" would crush the serpent's head, or, in other words, deliver a deathblow to Satan. So while the serpent defeats Adam and his offspring, the woman's seed and her offspring will defeat the serpent.

This is what Christ has done. Christ is the seed of the woman. He has defeated the devil.

Last Adam

Paul speaks of the same thing in 1 Corinthians 15:47:

> *The first man was of the dust of the earth, the second man from heaven.*

The first man was dust, and therefore was the serpent's food. But the second man, Jesus, was not dust, and therefore, Satan had no dominion over Him.

Notice that Paul calls Jesus the **second man**, yet he also calls Him the **last Adam**.

> *So it is written: "The first man Adam became a living being"; the last Adam, a life giving spirit." (1 Cor. 15:45)*

Jesus is not the second Adam; He is the last Adam. There is a big difference. If He were the second Adam, that would mean there would be other Adams who would represent humanity. Since He is the last Adam, there would be no other to come after Him. By being the last Adam, He ends the first

47

adamic race, with all of its defeat, sin, and failure, and becomes the sum total of the last Adamic race.

If Applewhite would have known that Jesus is the last Adam, he would not have been deceived into thinking that he was another Adam. This is one the errors of many cult leaders. They think that they are another Christ. But friend, there is only one Christ. He is called the **last Adam.** No more are to follow!

Jesus is not only the last Adam, but He is the second man. This means that He is the head of the new race of men. Just as the first Adam was the first man to represent humanity and become the head of the first race of humans, so Christ is the second man to head up the new race of humans. The Bible calls this new race "a new creation" (2 Cor. 5:17). Paul continues:

> As was the earthly man, so are those who are of the earth; and as is the man from heaven, so also are those who are heaven. And just as we have borne the likeness of the earthly man, so let us bear the likeness of the man from heaven. (1 Cor. 15:48-49, early manuscripts)

Do you see it? The first race was born on earth, and is dust and subject to the serpent. But the second race is born from heaven, and consequently has dominion over the serpent. Let us bear the likeness of Jesus' dominion over Satan.

Destroy Satan's Works

One of the main reasons that Jesus came was to take back for us what Satan stole from Adam. Jesus came to defeat the devil for us.

> ...The reason the Son of God appeared was to destroy the devil's work. (1 John 3:8)

Defeating the devil was not an afterthought with Christ; it was a main issue with Him. Jesus did not come to die for our sins and at the last minute, say, "While I'm at it, I might as well destroy the devil, also."

He had in mind from the beginning to defeat the devil. The Bible says that this was **the reason the Son of God appeared**. Most people say that Jesus came to die for our sins, and that is true. However, if Jesus provided forgiveness of sins without defeating the devil for us, we would have only a partial redemption. A complete redemption must include conquering Satan.

Jesus had on the forefront of his purpose to defeat the devil. This purpose is not minor, it is major. We should not downplay this part of redemption.

As far as the believer is involved, the devil's works are destroyed. The word **destroy** as found in the previous verse means to render ineffective and useless. Satan's works, which includes sickness, poverty, sin, and death are rendered ineffective and useless to you. They don't have power over your life anymore. You do not have to tolerate sickness, poverty, sin, and premature death in your life.

> *Since the children have flesh and blood, [Christ] too shared in their humanity so that by his death he might destroy him who holds the power of death—that is the devil—and free those who all their lives were held in slavery by their fear of death. (Hebrews 2:14-15)*

Jesus became incarnate for the direct purpose of destroying the power of the devil. The devil's power over you is destroyed. One translation of this verse says, "He might paralyze him" (RHM). It is unscriptural to say that Satan is alive and well on planet earth; instead, he is crippled and maimed—as far as the believer is concerned.

The New Creation

The final way that Jesus defeated the devil is through His body on earth—that is, the Church. It would be better stated that Jesus continues to defeat Satan through the new creation, which is us.

And God placed all things under his feet and appointed him to be head over everything for the church, which is his body...(Ephesians 1:22-23)

Notice the purpose of God placing all things, including Satan, under Christ's feet. The purpose is to give the Church authority over Satan. Christ's feet is attached to the body, not the head. The body is us. God wanted to rule the devil, not on His own, but through us. This is God's ultimate purpose.

God takes more delight in seeing us rule the devil than in Himself, alone, ruling the devil. In fact, this is the way that God defeats the devil. He defeats him through us.

This is what Paul meant in Romans 16:29: "The God of peace will soon crush Satan under our feet."

Who does the crushing? God does. How does He do the crushing? He crushes Satan **under our feet**. You see, God is working through His body, which is us. This is how God crushes Satan in our day. If you don't exercise authority over Satan, then God doesn't. God will exercise His authority when you do!

Do you remember the passage in Genesis 3:15 which mentions the offspring of the woman crushing Satan's head? Every Bible teacher I have ever heard always mentions that the **seed** or **offspring** of the woman is Christ. This is true, but only partially true.

According to Romans 16:29, the offspring of the woman is also the Church. It would be more accurate to say that the first born of the woman is Christ, and the rest of her offspring is us. Revelation chapter twelve confirms this:

A great and wondrous sign appeared in heaven: a woman clothed with the sun, with the moon under her feet and crown of twelve stars on her head. She was pregnant and cried out in pain as she was about to give birth...She gave birth to a son, a male child, who will rule all the nations with an iron scepter. And her child was snatched up to God and to his throne. (Rev. 12: 1-2, 5)

It is clear that the male child which the woman gave birth to is Christ. However, Revelation continues the story of the woman after Christ is taken up into heaven, which is after the ascension.

> *Then the dragon [Satan] was enraged at the woman and went off to make war against the rest of her offspring—those who obey God's commandments and hold to the testimony of Jesus. (v. 17)*

So you see that the woman in Genesis 3:15 has a first born Son, who is Jesus, but she also has more children after Christ is born. The rest of her offspring are those who confess Jesus as Lord—that's us! So Satan's battle now is with us, not with Christ.

More than a Conqueror

You may have been taught that the battle is the Lord's. It is true, the battle is the Lord's, but it is also ours. Let me explain.

God wanted to make us "more than conquerors" (Romans 8:37). I would have been happy if God just made me a conqueror. But He wanted me to be more than a conqueror.

What's the difference between being a conqueror and being "more than a conqueror"? Take a champion boxer, such as George Foreman, and put him into the ring. For the next twelve rounds he is going to put up a tough fight. He is going to be punched, bruised, cut, and bloodied during the fight. Yet, in the end, he wins. **George Foreman is a conqueror.**

After the fight, the promoters hands him a check for several millions of dollars. He smiles as he drives home. He walks into his home and embraces his beautiful wife. She looks George in the eyes and brags, "Oh, honey, you did such a wonderful job." She has compassion on her husband as she wipes away the puss and blood still dripping from the fight.

George lifts up the check to his wife and says, "Here's the money, honey." She grabs the check. **She is more than a conqueror.**

You see, Jesus did the fighting; so the battle is the

Lord's. He was the one whipped, bruised, cut, and bloodied. So through the cross, he defeated the devil. Then He smiles at us and says, "Enjoy the inheritance I purchased for you!"

The enemy has been beaten, and we enjoy the sacrifice that Christ went through for us. We are more than conquerors!

Seated with Christ

Not only is the devil defeated but the contest between the believer and Satan is not even close. The believer has far more authority over the devil than he usually realizes.

The book of Ephesians, perhaps more than any other book in the Bible, gives us a wonderful picture of our authority over Satan. In chapter 2, verse 6, it says:

And God raised us up with Christ and seated us with him in the heavenly realms in Christ Jesus.

Notice that this Scripture does not say that God "will someday in the future" raise us up. No, God has already **raised us up**. This verse is talking about a present reality, not a promise that God has yet to fulfill.

Where did God raise us up? The Bible says, **in the heavenly realms**. That is your position right now in Christ Jesus.

You may appear to be on planet earth; after all, you are in this world but you are not of it. You are of the heavenly places in Christ. You have been raised up, not by yourself, but with Christ. His exaltation is your exaltation.

If the Heaven's Gate cult would have known that they could be born again and be seated in heavenly places, they would not have desired to be caught up in a spaceship. Flying in a spaceship does not even compare to being seated with Christ in heavenly places.

God tells us how high we have been lifted up. In chapter 1, verse 20, it says:

which [God] *exerted in Christ when he raised him from the dead and seated him at his right hand in the heavenly*

realms, far above all rule and authority, power and domin-
ion, and every title that can be given, not only in the present
age but also in the one to come.

How high has Christ been exalted? He's been exalted **far above all rule and authority, power and dominion**. Not simply above, but far above. In other words, Christ is not even close to the rest of the rulers, authorities, and powers. He is far above them all. And that's where you are!

You are seated with Christ. He was not seated alone, but He took you along with Him and made you sit with Him. You don't have to wait for a spaceship to catch you up, you are already caught up in heavenly places with Christ.

In the mind of God, you are seated with Christ in heaven. You're not seated below Christ, but with Him. Since He is seated far above all rulers, guess what? You're seated with Christ, far above all rulers, authorities, and powers. That's where you are! You are seated in a position of authority far above the devil.

THE HEAVEN'S GATE SUICIDE

Chapter 5

Resist the Devil

There are always two sides to every battle and victory: God's side and man's side. God's side is what God accomplished for us in the redemption of Christ. It is an accomplished fact. It is legal. Man's side is what God is now doing in the believer through the weapons He gave him. This means that victory is not automatic.

The Bible teaches that the devil is defeated. You might assume since the devil is defeated that he can't harm you. He is legally defeated, yes! But it is your responsibility to apply the victory of Christ. There is no automatic immunity from Satan just because you're saved.

The Bible says, "They overcame [the devil] by the blood of the Lamb and by the word of their testimony" (Rev. 12:11). There were two weapons used to overcome Satan: the blood and the Word. The **blood** speaks of the redemption which Christ wrought for us on the cross. The **word of their testimony** is how they applied the blood. You cannot simply live a passive life. You must actively fight Satan.

Kenneth Hagin's Vision

Kenneth Hagin tells of a vision he had of Jesus. The Lord appeared to him and proceeded to teach him about how to deal with demons. As Jesus was speaking, a demon, who looked part monkey and human, walked between him and Jesus. The demon began to jump up and down in order to distract Kenneth. As the demon continued to do this, a dark cloud came between him and Jesus.

55

The demon began to yell in a high-pitch voice, "Yakety, yak yak! Yakety yak yak!" What disturbed Hagin the most was the fact that Jesus seemed totally oblivious to this demon. Jesus continued to talk as though the demon was not there.

Kenneth Hagin thought, "Doesn't Jesus know I can't hear what He's saying to me? Why doesn't Jesus tell this demon to stop?"

Finally in exasperation, and without really thinking about it, Brother Hagin pointed his finger at this demon and shouted, "I command you to cease and desist in Jesus' name!" The moment he said that, the demon fell on his face and hit the floor hard. The dark cloud disappeared. The demon laid on the floor, trembling and crying like a little puppy who was hit by a newspaper.

Jesus looked at Kenneth and glanced down at the demon and said while pointing at the demon, "If you hadn't done something about that evil spirit, I couldn't have!" Jesus proceeded to explain to him that the believer is the one with the authority to drive out spirits. Jesus continued, "To pray that I, the Lord Jesus Christ, or that God the Father would do anything about the devil is to waste your time."

You see, many believers are waiting for God to do something about the devil, when, in fact, Jesus delegated His authority to us. It is our responsibility to resist the devil and cast out demons. Nowhere do we find that the early church ever asked God to cast out demons or resist the devil for them. No, they always personally took authority over demons and cast them out themselves.

Jesus says, "And these signs will accompany those who believe: In my name they will drive out demons" (Mark 16:17). Who is to drive out demons? Not Jesus, but "they." They speaks of the believers. If you're a believer, then it is your responsibility to cast out demons. If you don't, then God won't.

Pick Up Your Sword

Kenneth Copeland had a similar vision to that of Kenneth Hagin. Brother Copeland was in Beaumont, Texas when God gave him a striking revelation through a vision. He was preparing for the service when suddenly he saw himself standing in the pulpit of the church. He looked up and saw a horrid dragon. It was repulsive. The dragon expanded like a balloon-filled float, yet it was alive. It was snorting fire and smoke. It turned on Copeland and almost burned his clothes.

He fell back to avoid the flames. As he was on his back, he saw Jesus standing nearby with a sword in His hand. Brother Copeland thought, "All right! Jesus is here to help me!" Yet, Jesus simply stood there doing nothing.

This got Copeland mad, "Why doesn't Jesus do something about this awful dragon? Can't he notice that I'm hurting?" But Jesus did not move. He stood there with a frown on His face, looking disappointed with Kenneth.

It dawned on Copeland that the sword Jesus was holding was for him to use on the dragon. He got up from the floor, ran to Jesus and took the sword. As he grabbed it, the sword lifted him from the floor. It had a power of its own. Then, with little effort, he touched the dragon's chin with the sword, and the dragon was split in two.

Many believers act like Kenneth Copeland before he took the sword. They're on their back—defeated by the devil. They're waiting for God to deliver them. Yet God is waiting for them to take the sword of the Spirit and use it on the devil.

Back to the Bible

You might say, "How can I be sure that these visions were really from God? I only believe in the Bible." Good, so do I. Let's look to the Bible and see how the early church dealt with the devil and demons.

> *[Jesus] called his twelve disciple to him and gave them authority to drive out evil spirits and to heal every disease and sickness. (Matt. 10:1)*

Who had the authority to drive out spirits? The apostles had the authority. It was their duty to drive out spirits. They were not to ask Jesus to do it for them. They were to do it.

You might say, "Yes, that authority belonged to the apostles, but not to us." If your right, then we don't have authority over spirits, consequently, we are vulnerable to them. Let me show you that Jesus expanded this authority to more than the twelve apostles.

After this the Lord appointed seventy-two others and sent them two by two ahead of him to every town and place where he was about to go... (Luke 10:1)

Look at the result of their mission:

The seventy-two returned with joy and said, "Lord, even the demons submit to us in your name. (Luke 10:17)

They exercised authority over spirits. These were not the apostles; these were seventy-two disciples. The number seventy-two is significant. It was seventy-two elders who prophesied along with Moses. When they did, Moses declared,

... "I wish that all the LORD'S people were prophets and that the LORD would put his Spirit on them!" (Num. 11:29)

Moses was prophesying our day. The number seventy-two speaks of God's desire to put His Spirit on all people, so that all may have power over demons. The seventy-two which Jesus appointed are the representatives of all the body of Christ. Their ability is our ability. What they could do, all believers can do. To prove this, look at Jesus words before He ascended:

Jesus said to them, "Go into all the world and preach the good news to all creation. Whoever believes and is baptized will be saved, but whoever does not believe will be condemned. And these signs will accompany those who believe: In my name they will drive out demons... (Mark 16:15-17)

Jesus said that these signs will accompany **those who**

believe. He did not say that these signs will accompany only apostles. No, these signs accompany anyone who believes. Are you a believer? If yes, then these signs should accompany you, including the sign to drive out demons.

Tradition has talked believers out of expelling demons. They think they don't have the authority, or else they think demons have gone out of existence, or worse, they're waiting for God to cast out demons. In reading much of the Christian literature you get the impression that demons don't exist, or that they have been huddled in dark regions away from us educated people.

Friend, demons do exist and you have authority over them, but you must exercise your authority by commanding them to leave. If you don't, then they'll hang around you.

The Devil Will Flee

The Epistles confirm that the believer must personally take authority over the devil:

> *Submit yourselves, then, to God. Resist the devil, and he will flee from you. (James 4:7)*

> *Be self-controlled and alert. Your enemy the devil prowls around like a roaring lion looking for someone to devour. Resist him, standing firm in the faith... (1 Pet. 4:8-9)*

Both these Scriptures confirm the fact that it is the obligation of the believer to **resist the devil**. Resist means to violently oppose. The result of this will be that the devil will flee from you. Flee means to run in stark terror. The devil is afraid of the believer who knows how to resist him. This is why he wants to convince you to do nothing about him.

The Devil's Foothold

> *and do not give the devil a foothold. (Ep. 4:27)*

"You" is the understood subject. "You are not to give the devil a foothold." It is not God's duty to keep the devil out of your life—it is yours'!

"Well, I'm trusting the Lord that He will keep the devil from attacking me."

You're wrong. I'm glad you trust the Lord, but that "trust" must be activated through your taking authority over the devil. Many people have a passive faith—they believe everything that happens to them is God's will. That kind of faith will get you in trouble. You need to understand that the devil will try to attack you, and if you do nothing about him, then he will succeed.

Resist Sickness

The devil has placed sicknesses on many believers. In some cases, these diseases will take their lives. And many are simply waiting to die, thinking that they are powerless over sickness.

Jesus not only gave you authority to drive out demons, but He has given you authority to heal the sick. Don't accept sickness as the will of God. Realize that the devil is the author of sickness and disease. Resist him, and he will flee from you.

I'm tired of seeing the devil walk all over believers. He doesn't have the right to tread on you. But he will if you accept the traditional ideas that sickness is from God, or is used of God to teach you. God does not use the devil as a schoolmaster. He hates his guts. He can't stand what he's done to His children.

Then why doesn't God do something about him? He has! He's given you His power and authority so that you can cast him out.

Many believers are going to heaven with sickness, asking God why He didn't heal them. God is answering them, "I gave you my Word, Name, and Power to heal the sick and drive out demons. But you were waiting for Me to do more. What else could I have done? I gave you everything you needed to win the battle over sickness and the devil. And you stood there waiting for Me to do what you were to do!"

Friend, take this message to heart! Resist the devil, and God guarantees that he will flee from you!

THE HEAVEN'S GATE SUICIDE

Chapter 6

Who Are the True Heaven's Gate Keepers?

I will give you the keys of the kingdom of heaven; whatever you bind on earth will be bound in heaven, and whatever you loose on earth will be loosed in heaven.
—*Matthew 16:19*

Undoubtedly, the Heaven's Gate cult based their name on this passage of Scripture. It is sad that they did not really understand the true meaning of this passage. To them, this passage meant that all people had to come to them to be able to enter the kingdom of heaven which they interpreted to mean a "literal and physical Heavens."

What does this passage really mean?

Jesus is saying that heaven will bind what you bind, and will loose what you loose. The words **bind** and **loose** means to "not allow" and to "allow". In other words, heaven will allow whatever you allow, and it will disallow whatever you disallow.

People often question God when tragedy happens, "Why did God allow it?"

The answer is because God has given us, the Church, the power to not allow what is of the devil. A lot of things which happen are caused by the devil. You can't blame God for what the devil does.

You say, "But why did God allow the devil to do this terrible thing?" Because God gave us the keys to stop him. God is not responsible to stop the devil. We are! It is our responsibility to bind the devil.

If the Church knew about the Heaven's Gate cult and

did not take authority over the lying spirits over their lives, then the Church is responsible to a certain degree for this tragedy. The Church is the true guards over "Heaven's Gate." We have the keys of the kingdom to bind the devil.

What Can You Bind?

Some theologians limit the usage of binding and loosing to church authority. They confine the concept of binding to excommunication. Undoubtedly this is part of what the word bind means, however the New Testament expands on the usage of the word bind to also include binding the devil. Earlier in Matthew's gospel Jesus mentions about binding Satan:

> *Or else how can one enter into a strong man's house, and spoil his goods, except he first bind the strong man? And then he will spoil his house. (Matt. 12:29, KJV)*

The **strong man** is Satan. He's mentioned in the preceding verses.

> *If Satan drives out Satan, he is divided against himself. (Matt. 12:26).*

So Jesus describes Himself as the One who **binds** the strong man. The word bind is the Greek word *deo* and is found in both passages, first about us using the keys to bind and second about the Lord binding the strong man.

This Greek word is also used in connection with the devil making people sick. After healing a woman with curvature of the spine, Jesus said,

> *Then should not this woman, a daughter of Abraham, whom Satan has kept bound for eighteen long years, be set free on the Sabbath day from what bound her? (Luke 13:16).*

Jesus described this sick woman as being **bound** by Satan. The word bound is the same word as used in the previous verses.

In Revelation chapter 20 the same Greek word is used in conjunction with Satan being bound for a thousand years.

> *And I saw an angel coming down out of heaven, having the key to the Abyss and holding in his hand a great chain. He seized the dragon, that ancient serpent, who is the devil, or Satan, and bound him for a thousand years. (Rev. 20:1-2)*

The angel **bound** Satan with a key. The word bound is the word *deo*, the same word found in the other verses. It's clear, then, that the authority Christ gave us to bind can be applied to binding the devil.

Who Has the Keys?

Let's go back to the passage in Matthew 16:19 about the power to bind and loose. Some people will point out that Jesus was speaking to Peter about the keys of the kingdom, and as a result have assumed that Peter was the sole possessor of the keys of the kingdom.

It is true that Jesus first gave the keys to Peter, but later he gave the keys to all the disciples. Notice what Jesus said to all the disciples,

> *I tell you [twelve] the truth, whatever you bind on earth will be bound in heaven, and whatever you loose on earth will be loosed in heaven. (Matt. 18:18)*

This statement is the exact statement which was made originally to Peter. So Peter was not the sole possessor of the keys. The other disciples received the keys as well.

Most people totally misunderstand what the keys of the kingdom can do. Religionists, especially those who claim apostolic succession, think that Jesus was giving Peter and perhaps all the apostles the right to include or exclude people from heaven. This was of course the view of Applewhite. He believed that he was the one who determined if people could go to heaven. However, this is not what this Scripture is teaching.

Keys Work on Earth

Instead of jumping to conclusions concerning the power of the keys of the kingdom, we should allow Jesus to tell us what the keys can do. Let's look once again at the words Jesus spoke to Peter:

> *I will give you the keys of the kingdom of heaven; whatever you bind on earth will be bound in heaven... (Matt. 16:19)*

These keys are used to bind whatever is on **earth**. You can't use these keys to bind things in heaven; they only have power to bind things on the earth. Heaven will back up whatever you bind, but you can only bind what is on earth. So you can clearly see that these keys have nothing to do with allowing or disallowing people to enter heaven.

Keys Give Dominion

Keys represent ownership, which translates to authority and power. Just recently I purchased a house. After closing the deal I was given the keys. This meant that I now had the legal right and power to move into my home.

When Jesus said, "I will give you the keys," He meant, "I will give you authority and power to allow or disallow whatever is on earth."

Jesus used the term "kingdom of heaven" to refer to God's sovereign rule over the world. Many people mistakenly confuse this term with "heaven." Heaven is the spiritual place that you go to when you die. This is not the same as the kingdom of heaven.

Jesus often used parables to describe the kingdom of heaven, and none of His parables could be interpreted to mean heaven in the sky where people go after they die. And it definitely is not a physical place you go to by committing suicide. The kingdom of heaven is simply God's power and authority. "The kingdom of God is not a matter of talk but of power" (1

Cor. 4:20). God's kingdom is His power. They mean the same. This means that Jesus was giving us God's heavenly authority and power to bring about God's will on earth.

Keys are Plural

I was reading this Scripture about the keys of the kingdom when the Lord spoke to me. He said, "Did you notice that the word 'keys' is plural?"

I answered, "No, Lord, I've never noticed that before!"

The Lord continued, "The trouble with my people is that they try to bind and loose with only one key. I gave them more than one key. They should use all the keys that I gave them."

I asked, "Lord, how many keys did you give us?"

He answered by reminding me of Acts 4:29-31. There I found the three keys of the kingdom.

> *Now, Lord, consider their threats and enable your servants to speak your **word** with great boldness. Stretch out your hand to heal and perform miraculous signs and wonders through the **name** of your holy servant Jesus." After they prayed, the place where they were meeting was shaken. And they were all filled with the **Holy Spirit** and spoke the word of God boldly. [Emphasis added]*

I saw it! Joy filled my heart as I recognized these three keys: the Word of God, the name of Jesus, and the Holy Spirit.

You need all three keys to exercise dominion over the devil. You cannot employ just one key and think that everything is going to be all right. You need all three keys.

While I meditated on this the Lord began to make these things very clear to me. As I thought about these keys, I realized that they represent the three branches of God's government. The kingdom of heaven is God's government.

> *For to us a child is born, to us a son is given, and the government will be on his shoulders...Of the increase of his gov-*

ernment and peace there will be no end. He will reign on David's throne and over his kingdom..." (Is. 9:6-7).

Notice that Jesus upholds **his government**. Don't misread this. He does not uphold human governments. Jesus has His own government. It is His kingdom. The keys of the kingdom are the branches of His government. And these keys are how He rules.

Most human governments have three branches: legislative, judicial, and executive. In the United States the legislative branch is the Congress. They make the laws. The Supreme Court is the judicial branch. They give authority to the laws. And then there is the President. He is the executive branch. He enforces the laws.

With those three branches in mind, you can easily see the way God's government—His kingdom—operates. The Word of God is the legislative branch. The Name of Jesus is the judicial branch. And the Holy Spirit is the executive branch.

Legislative Branch

God's legislative branch is the Word of God. What can you bind and loose? The words bind and loose were legal terms in Jesus' day. The word bind meant to declare unlawful and the word loose meant to declare lawful. You find out from the Word of God what is lawful and unlawful. The first thing you need to know in order to exercise dominion over the devil is the law.

For example, the first thing a police officer must know in order to enforce the law is to know the law itself. How can he enforce the law if he does not know what the law says?

The same is true of you. How can you bind Satan if you don't know the law, which is the Word of God? You won't know what is unlawful for Satan if you don't know what the Word of God says.

Many people try to exercise dominion over the devil when he brings sickness, poverty, and temptation. But without knowing the Word of God, these people will be defeated. When they face sickness, they say, "Devil, take your sickness with you and leave my life!"

Yet the devil says, "Why should I leave! I don't have to obey you!" At this point, many sincere Christians don't know what Scriptures to use against the devil. They don't know what the Word of God says about sickness and divine health.

When Jesus was tempted, He simply said, "It is written!" Can you say to the devil, "It is written!"?

"Well, that's my problem. I don't know what the Bible says."

You definitely have a problem. You see, the devil is not afraid of you personally. He is afraid of God. "You believe that there is one God. Good! Even the demons believe that—and shudder" (James 2:19).

The devil and demons are afraid of God. If you can't tell them what God has said, then they will hang around you because they are not afraid of you.

Several years back, our church met in a building where we shared utility lines with another tenant. Without getting into a long story, the tenant in order to get revenge at our church turned off the water. Unfortunately, the water line was inside his side of the building.

We called the police, and they sent an officer. We told him the problem. He walked over to this tenant and asked him, "Did you turn off the water?"

"Yes."

"Would you please turn it back on?"

He answered, "No." The officer was shocked but could do nothing.

He told me, "Pastor, I have no jurisdiction over the water utilities. The authority over the water belongs to the water company."

I had called the wrong person. The police could not operate in another's jurisdiction. Now, the police officer had the power to make the man do anything. He had a gun, a club, and handcuffs. But he could not use his power without the law giving him permission.

You see, the only jurisdiction which has authority over the devil is God Word. He listens to His Word only. No other word will make the devil obey.

I am surprised how many Christians try to help people

out of the cults by trying to use psychological means, instead of using the Word of God. Can't we learn from the Branch Davidians that no amount of psychological manipulation is going to free people from Satan's power. Only God's Word can drive Satan out.

Judicial Branch

The second branch of God's kingdom is the judicial branch. It has authority to make decisions based on the law. God's judicial branch is Jesus Christ. God established Him as the judge. "For [God] has set a day when he will judge the world with justice by the man he has appointed. He has given proof of this to all men by raising him from the dead" (Acts 17:31).

The United States Supreme Court is made up of judges. They interpret the law. Jesus Christ is the interpreter of God's Word. His interpretation is the final authority on all matters of Bible interpretation. I'm surprised to see many believers depart from Jesus' interpretation in order to establish their own interpretations of the Bible. For example, Jesus says,

> *In solemn truth I tell you, anyone believing in me shall do the same miracles I have done, and even greater ones, because I am going to be with the Father. (John 14:12, Living Bible)*

Despite the clear promise of Christ, many churches deny the role of miracles for today. I hear preachers say, "I believe God can heal, but I don't believe in faith healers."

What they mean by "faith healers" are those who lay hands on the sick like Jesus did in Bible times. Would Jesus be considered a "faith healer"? If a faith healer is someone who believes that God can heal **through** him, then we all ought to be faith healers.

Critics of present day miracles interpret the Scriptures about the believer possessing miracle powers in light of their denominational tradition. Instead, they should interpret those Scriptures in light of Christ's authority. And He clearly interpreted the Word of God as teaching that all believers may possess God's supernatural power to work miracles. This example is a good case in point that shows how Christians have departed from the authority of God's Supreme Court Justice, Jesus Christ.

The thing that baffles people regarding Herff Applewhite was that he grew up in church. People don't understand why he did not want anything to do with his church. Friend, with all do respect, the problem with his church and churches like his, is that they lack the power of God. Many church men have deprived God's Word of its power by relying on their interpretation, instead of accepting the clear teachings of the Bible.

Let's face it: How many churches really believe in divine healing, miracles, and tongues? Not too many, yet they claim to believe in the Bible. There is a contradiction in what they claim to believe in and the Bible itself.

If the Church wants to keep people from following fanatical cults, then she better start preaching the Word of God with power, and believe for great miracles, or else, the people are going to look for spiritual experiences that they could not find in their church.

So in the end, you can read and memorize and claim to preach all the Scriptures, but if you reject Jesus Christ clear teachings then you have lost one of the keys to bind the devil. You will have made the mistake of the theologians in Jesus' day. He told them, "Woe to you experts in the law, because you have taken away the key to knowledge. You yourselves have not entered, and you have hindered those who were entering" (Luke 11:52).

This is true for today. Many sincere people are trying to enter into all the fullness of the gospel—tongues, healing, faith, gifts of the Spirit, spiritual warfare—yet traditional churches hinder these hungry disciples from pursuing the Spirit-filled life. After they are discouraged from having these biblical experiences, they search for a cult that will give them the spiritual experiences they are hungry for. Unfortunately, they are receiving the counterfeit experiences.

Authority

The name of Jesus gives us the experiences we are looking for. Through His name we have authority to drive out
demons and work miracles. Jesus says,

> ... *"Go into all the world and preach the good news to all
> creation. Whoever believes and is baptized will be saved, but
> whoever does not believe will be condemned. And these signs
> will accompany those who believe: In my name they will drive
> out demons; they will speak in new tongues; they will pick up
> snakes with their hands; and when they drink deadly poison,
> it will not hurt them at all; they will place their hands on
> sick people, and they will get well." (Mark 16:15-18)*

How will believers do these miracles? Jesus says, **"In my
name."** We do them in Jesus' name. You can speak the Word of
God and get some results. But you will get better results when
you speak the Word **in the name of Jesus.** Demons listen to the
name of Jesus.

Do you obey the speed limit laws? You might qualify
your answer by saying, "Yes, well, yes, if I see a police car." It's
amazing how slow we can drive when we see a police car.

You see, a police car represents authority. Notice that
authority will make people obey the laws. People drive past the
speed limit signs all the time, and many refuse to obey what the
speed limit laws say. Demons act like this.

You can quote many Scriptures, but they will ignore you
until you show them authority. The authority you have is in the
name of Jesus. When you say, "In the name of Jesus, the Word
of God says this!" the demons listen and obey. They are like the
drivers ignoring the speed limit laws until they see someone
with authority.

Do you know the authority that you have in the name of
Jesus? The name of Jesus is your badge of authority.

A police officer can stand at an intersection and direct
traffic. He lifts his hand and blows the whistle at the drivers
going one direction, and those drivers stop. Now listen: the one
hundred and eighty pound police officer has no power to stop

a two-ton car, but the drivers stop because the police officer has authority.

When you confidently show your badge of authority to the devil he obeys. Your badge is the name of Jesus.

The disciples recognized the authority they had in Christ. They said to Jesus, "Lord, even the demons submit to us in your name" (Luke 10:17). In essence they were saying, "The demons know that You are the Supreme Court Justice of the kingdom. They obey us when we use Your authority!"

Joint Heirs With Christ

Most people don't understand what it means to use Jesus' name. His name is not a magic wand. The seven sons of Sceva tried to use Jesus' name in this way, and as a result they got beaten up by a demon possessed man (Acts 19:13-16).

A name is only as good as the person himself. If I handed you a check of a million dollars would you be excited? It all depends if I had a million dollars. I can sign over my name to you, and it would be worth the value of my riches.

To understand the name of Jesus, you have to understand the wealth and authority of Jesus. You must know what is invested in the name of Jesus.

Power of Attorney

E.W. Kenyon did a teaching along this line when a lawyer interrupted him, "Are you saying that Jesus gave us the power of attorney?"

Mr. Kenyon said, "Sir, you're the lawyer. I'm only a preacher. You tell me. Did Jesus give us the power of attorney?"

The lawyer pointed to the Bible said, "If words mean anything, then Jesus definitely gave us the power of attorney."

"Then tell me brother," Kenyon asked, "What is the value of having the power of attorney?"

"It all depends on the wealth of the individual. If the individual is wealthy, then the person with the power of attorney is wealthy."

Praise God! Jesus is wealthy! And since He's wealthy, so are you!

Go through the Gospels and find out everything that Christ did. What He did, His name can do through you. His name on your lips can do everything He can do!

Chapter 7

Did They Speak in Tongues?

We now come to the final branch of God's governmental kingdom—the executive branch. Laws and authority are great, but they mean very little if there is no power to enforce the laws.

The Supreme court, through their authority, struck down segregation. Nevertheless, many racists refused to allow minorities into their schools, businesses, and organizations. Who came to the aid of the minorities? Not the Supreme Court Justices—but the President. He sent the military to ensure the rights of minorities.

You see, it is not the job of Christ to enforce the Word of God over the devil, because it's the assignment of the Holy Spirit to enforce God's Word. Christ, Himself, said, "I drive out demons by the Spirit of God" (Matt. 12:28). Jesus declared that His miracles were done by God's power, not by His own power. Jesus said, "By myself I can do nothing" (John 5:30). Jesus never did a miracle until He was filled with the Holy Spirit.

The Holy Spirit is the executive branch. He is the One with the **power**. Christ is the One with the **authority**. The name of Jesus gives you authority and the Holy Spirit gives you power. You must drive out demons by the authority of the name of Jesus through the power of the Holy Spirit.

Jesus said to His disciples, after giving them authority to drive out demons,

> ...*Do not leave Jerusalem, but wait for the gift my Father promised...you will receive power when the Holy Spirit comes on you...(Acts 1:4,8)*

Jesus did not say that they would receive **authority**, but He said that they would receive **power** when the Holy Spirit came on them. The Bible always uses power in conjunction with the Holy Spirit. He is the One with the power of God.

Just like the disciples needed the power of the Holy Spirit in their lives, we, too, need that same power. We must receive the Spirit in the same way that they did. No other way will do.

Bible Experience

Acts 2:1-4 describes their experience of receiving the Holy Spirit,

> *When the day of Pentecost came, they were all together in one place. Suddenly a sound like the blowing of a violent wind came from heaven and filled the whole house where they were sitting. They saw what seemed to be tongues of fire that separated and came to rest on each of them. All of them were filled with the Holy Spirit and began to speak in other tongues as the Spirit enabled them.*

Never settle for anything less than what the early church experienced. Today, traditional Christians have not usually experienced the same power that the early church experienced.

For example, many Catholics seem satisfied to have a little oil on their head as their evidence of receiving the Holy Spirit. However, a glance at this incident shows that this was no Confirmation Sacrament. Oil will never suffice for the real power of God.

Protestant doctrine has been even more of a hindrance for Protestants to receive the Holy Spirit. One good thing about the Catholic doctrine as opposed to Protestant theology is that they teach baptism and confirmation as two separate sacraments. Confirmation is the sacrament where the baptized candidate receives the Holy Spirit. This has helped me share with Catholics about receiving the Holy Spirit. They can easily relate to the two experiences of the New Birth (baptism) and the Baptism in the Holy Spirit. I don't have to explain or prove to them that salvation and the baptism in the Holy Spirit are two separate experiences. Consequently, I have led multitudes of Catholics into the genuine baptism in the Holy Spirit with the evidence of speaking in tongues.

The problem is with Protestants. They seem content with the experience of the new birth and water baptism. Many are taught that there is no other spiritual experience after water baptism. Unfortunately, they are taught wrong.

Applewhite Wanted a Spiritual Experience

If Herff Applewhite had received the Holy Spirit in his church, I wonder if he would had turned to receiving an evil spirit. I don't think so. Receiving the Holy Spirit is so wonderful that you won't want anything else.

It seems clear from Applewhite's writings that he wanted a spiritual experience. Instead of his church providing it for him, the devil did. Satan gave him another spirit. This spirit, Applewhite, claimed gave him the gift of tongues. But when he used the term tongues, he did not mean the scriptural use of languages which enabled him to "utter mysteries with his spirit" (1 Cor. 14:2).

To Applewhite, the tongues he received was "to speak in several languages and to several stratas simultaneously." One of his student's, called Jwnody, describes tongues in the following Website posting:

> Our dilemma was multifaceted: How do we present the information in a credible fashion, when to most, our Truth is definitely stranger than any fiction? How do we avoid being seen as religious, in order to not "turn off" those who rightfully despise the hypocrisy of what religions have become? At the same time, how do we acknowledge our past associations with this civilization which are primarily recorded in your Bible, so as to offer those who are waiting for prophecy to be fulfilled, enough clues to put it together? As you read our various presentations, you will see our many attempts to "speak in tongues"

As you can see, Applewhite and his cult considered tongues to mean a mixture of philosophies and various ways to preach their message, not the biblical understanding of tongues.

The church Applewhite was raised in did not teach him to receive the Holy Spirit in the same way as the early church received. His church did not teach the baptism in the Holy Spirit as a separate experience from salvation, consequently, he never had an opportunity to receive the genuine gift of the Holy Spirit. The Bible clearly teaches two separate spiritual experiences:

> But when [the Samaritans] believed Philip as he preached the good news of the kingdom of God and the name of Jesus Christ, they were baptized, both men and women...When the apostles in Jerusalem heard that Samaria had accepted the word of God, they sent Peter and John to them. When they arrived, they prayed for them that they might receive the Holy Spirit, because the Holy Spirit had not yet come upon any of them; they had simply been baptized into the name of the Lord Jesus. Then Peter and John placed their hands on them, and they received the Holy Spirit. (Acts 8:12, 14-17)

Could anyone rightly say that these Samaritans were not true Christians before Peter and John had come to them? They had every evidence of being genuine Christians: they believed the gospel; they accepted the Word of God; they proved their faith by being baptized. This is exactly the manner of conversion for evangelicals today. But unlike the early Church, today's evangelicals stop with water baptism.

The early church knew that the Samaritans lacked one important experience: the baptism in the Holy Spirit. This is true of many sincere followers of Christ today. They lack the baptism in the Holy Spirit.

It does not matter what you have been taught. Search the Scriptures and you will see that the baptism in the Holy Spirit is a separate experience from being born again. Receive this experience. You have no chance to successfully battle the devil without it. After all, Christ did not go into the desert to combat Satan until He had first received the Spirit.

> *When all the people were being baptized, Jesus was baptized too. And as he was praying, heaven was opened and the Holy Spirit descended on him in bodily form like a dove...Jesus full of the Holy Spirit, returned from the Jordan and was led by the Spirit in the desert, where for forty days he was tempted by the devil... (Luke 3:21-22, 4:1-2)*

Jesus was as much the Son of God before He was baptized and filled with the Spirit as He was afterward. You are as much a child of God before you were baptized and filled with the Spirit as you were afterward. However, as in the case of Jesus, you are not prepared to confront the devil until you are filled with the Spirit.

If Christ needed the Holy Spirit to confront Satan, then surely we all need the Holy Spirit to confront him as well.

Don't Stop There

Many Charismatics and Pentecostals stop with the baptism in the Holy Spirit. They think that they have all there is to have. This would be true if they **stayed** filled with the Holy Spirit. Unfortunately, as D.L. Moody once said, "The reason we need to keep being filled with the Spirit is because our vessels leak."

The Bible admonishes the full gospel Christians at Ephesus to "be filled with the Spirit" (Ep. 5:18). As a Pentecostal I was taught that when I had received the Holy Spirit that I had received the fullness of the Spirit permanently. It was true that I was filled with the Spirit when I had spoken in tongues, however, the Bible makes it clear that I must maintain the Spirit-filled life.

Just because you once spoke in tongues does not mean that you are constantly filled with the Spirit. The same book of Acts which convinced me that I needed to be initially filled with the Spirit, also taught me that I needed to stay filled with the Spirit.

79

In Acts 4:31 it says, "...And they were all filled with the Holy Spirit and spoke the word of God boldly." Who were **they** that were filled with the Spirit? **They** were the apostles and the rest of the disciples. They had already been filled with the Spirit on the day of Pentecost, so this was another infilling. This shows that they needed to stay filled with the Holy Spirit.

There is a refilling of the Spirit that many Pentecostals know nothing about. The reason you need to be refilled is because you get drained through the trials of life. Every time you encounter a trial, the power of God in you is released from you to help you overcome each trial. As a result, you are less filled after each trial, unless you refill your spiritual life through reading the Word, prayer, and fasting.

Paul on the Island of Malta

There is a great example in the Bible of this truth in action. It's the story of Paul on the Island of Malta. He arrived on the Island as a result of a shipwreck. For many days, he and all the people on board were in danger of losing their lives as a result of a terrible and lengthy storm. But Paul had faith that they would be safe, and they were. The ship was destroyed; however, all the people swam safely to the Island, some with the help of planks.

Paul's trials were not over, yet. Paul was warming himself by a fire when he reached to grab some brushwood to rekindle the flame. As he reached for the brushwood, a poisonous viper bit Paul. Paul knew the words of Christ which said that he could take up serpents and that no poison would hurt him. He stood on God's Word and suffered no ill effects.

This miracle caused the islanders to treat Paul hospitably, and they even welcomed him to the home of the chief official.

[The official's] *father was sick in bed, suffering from fever and dysentery. Paul went in to see him and, after prayer, placed his hands on him and healed him. (Acts 28:8)*

I was reading this when I noticed something unusual. Notice that Paul did not place his hands on the man until he had first prayed. The Bible says that **after prayer** Paul placed his hands on him. It hit me!

Paul was so drained spiritually through the long storm and by the snake bite that he was not ready to quickly lay hands on this man. Paul needed to pray first. And after he had prayed, he was ready to heal the man. Paul was refilling his life with spiritual power through prayer. After sufficiently praying, he was ready to exercise his spiritual power to heal the man.

I wonder how many of us are wise enough to spend time in prayer before we exercise a spiritual feat. Prayer refills our lives with the power of God, so that we have the power necessary to overcome Satan's works.

Prayer and Fasting

You might recall the incident when the disciples were not able to drive out a spirit. After Jesus had driven it out, the disciples asked him,

> ... *"Why couldn't we drive it out?"*
> *(Matt. 17:19)*

Notice that they **couldn't** drive it out. The word couldn't implies lack of ability, not lack of authority. They tried to use the authority of the name of Jesus, but the name was not sufficient in this case. So after explaining the power of faith, Jesus said,

> *"However, this kind does not go out except by prayer and fasting"* (Matt. 17:21, NKJV)

Jesus was warning the disciples that His name sometimes does not work without prayer and fasting. This was the case for these disciples. Instead of spending time praying, they were wasting it arguing over religion with the skeptics (Mk. 9:14). All the amount of arguing religion with cults wont's help them. You need to pray for them.

Jesus, on the other hand, had spent time on the Mountain of Transfiguration, praying and fasting. So He was prepared with power to cast out the demon.

There are certain demons which will not submit to the name of Jesus. I know that sounds almost blasphemous, but it's true. Some spirits are so rebellious, that only **power** is going to drive them out of people. And the way to get this power is through prayer and fasting.

Tumor Gone!

There was an incident in our church that illustrates the power of fasting. The Guillens were a bright, young, cheerful couple—cheerful despite the fact that their daughter was born with a large lump on the side of her neck. The child was beautiful, but the massive growth drew attention away from her pretty features.

Along with our church, they prayed diligently for her healing. Yet their prayers, including ours, did not seem to avail.

Then one day I received a call from this couple, "Pastor, out little girl is healed! The growth is gone!" The next day they shared their wonderful testimony with our church. With my own eyes I could verify this healing. There she was—perfectly healed! No trace of the growth was there.

The thing that impressed me the most was not the healing, but how the healing took place. This was the Guillens' testimony:

"The Lord laid upon our hearts to fast for our daughter. We didn't know much about fasting but we did it anyway. The moment we began to fast, our daughter began to complain that her neck was hurting. Soon she was screaming in pain. The soft growth turned hard. We were concerned, but we knew that God had called us to fast for our daughter, and we knew she would be healed. One morning we noticed that the growth was a little smaller. The next day it shank more. Finally, the growth disappeared altogether."

The thing that struck me the most about this testimony was the Guillens' fast. I'm convinced that their fasting produced the healing. Fasting increased the power of God in their lives so that they were able to drive out the tumor from their daughter.

Sometimes you need to fast and pray for those in the cults.

The Word, the Name, the Spirit

You have been given the three keys of the kingdom. I'm not sure that you have noticed this by now, but the three keys represent the three persons of the Trinity: the Word of God, the **Father**; the Name of **Jesus** His Son; and the Power of the **Holy Spirit**. By having a relationship with the fullness of the Godhead, you are given the three keys of the kingdom.

In the beginning we see the Trinity talking to humanity: "Let us make man in our image." God calls Himself "us." **Us** is plural, and speaks of the Trinity. The first words that the Trinity spoke to mankind was a blessing.

> *God blessed them and said unto them, Be fruitful, and multiply, and replenish the earth, and subdue it: and have dominion... (Gen. 1:28 KJV)*

The last words Jesus spoke to humanity was also a blessing.

> *When [Jesus] had led them out to the vicinity of Bethany, he lifted up his hands and blessed them. (Luke 24:20)*

The **blessing** is recorded in the Great Commission. In the Great Commission Jesus said to make disciples of all nations by baptizing them in the name of the Father, Son, and Holy Spirit, and through God's power they were to cast out demons, heal the sick, and do miracles.

Do you see the connection between the first Great Commission in Genesis and with the last Great Commission in the Gospels? The Trinity **blesses** God's followers with **dominion**. Dominion is having both the power and authority to govern and control.

And through the power of the Godhead—the three keys of God's government—you can successfully win the gorilla war against the devil, fallen angels, and demons.

Heaven's Gate Denied the Trinity

The terrible error of the Heaven's Gate cult was that they claimed to have the keys of the Kingdom, yet they denied the Trinity.

As far as God the Father was concerned, they believed that He was simply an "Older Member of the Evolutionary Level Above Human." In other words, they denied God as the Creator of the entire universe. By doing so they blasphemed God!

Concerning Jesus, in their minds, He was only a man until an alien entity entered Him when He was baptized by John the Baptist. At that time, according to them, He began the "metamorphic transition...from human to Level Above Human." However, the Bible says about Jesus Christ that "...by him all things were created: things in heaven and on earth, visible and invisible, whether thrones or powers or rulers or authorities; all things were created by him and for him" (Col. 1:16). Jesus is God! A denial of that keeps a person out of the true kingdom of God.

Not only did they blasphemed God and Jesus, but they blasphemed the Holy Spirit. Jesus said,

> *"Anyone who speaks a word against the Son of Man will be forgiven, but anyone who speaks against the Holy Spirit will not be forgiven, either in this age or in the age to come."* (Matt. 12:32)

Who did the Heaven's Gate members say that the Holy Spirit was? To them, He was one of the "crew of members of the Kingdom of Heaven who are responsible for nurturing 'gardens.'" The Holy Spirit is simply a crew member who appeared on earth 2,000 years ago! Can you believe it!?

The Bible tells us that the Holy Spirit is the third person of the Trinity. This group denied this biblical belief.

As you can see, although this cult claimed to have the keys of the Kingdom of Heaven, they denied the Trinity Who gives the keys. According to 1 John 2:22, they were the antichrists:

> *Who is the liar? It is the man who denies that Jesus is the Christ. Such a man is the antichrist—he denies the Father and the Son.*

THE HEAVEN'S GATE SUICIDE

Chapter 8

The Open Door

Marshal Herff Applewhite claimed that two alien spirits came to live in him and his wife, Bonnie Lu Trusdal Nettles, around 1970. Little by little, these spirits began to convince them that they were the same kind of spirits that entered Jesus at His baptism.

At first these spirits must have disturbed them, because they changed their names to Bo and Peep, after the nursery rhyme of the "Little Lost Sheep." After awhile, they did not feel like lost sheep, on the contrary, they believed that they were the shepherds for all the world. They eventually called these spirits Do and Ti. They were the new messiahs. Eventually, in 1985, Ti "left her human vehicle" to board a spaceship; Bonnie Nettle's had graduated.

The Heaven's Gate cult were demon possessed. It's that simple. The complicated part comes in how they became demon possessed. No one becomes demon possessed over night. Let me show you a dramatic case of demon possession in the Bible:

When Jesus stepped ashore, he was met by a demon-possessed man from the town. For a long time this man had not worn clothes or lived in a house, but had lived in the tombs. When he saw Jesus, he cried out and fell at his feet, shouting at the top of his voice, "What do you want with me, Jesus, Son of the Most High God? I beg you, don't torture me?" For Jesus had commanded the evil spirit to come out of the man. Many times it had seized him, and though he was chained hand and foot and kept under guard, he had broken his chains and had been driven by the demon into solitary places." (Luke 8:27-29)

This is the most dramatic case of demon possession in the Bible. In it we discover several facts about demons.

First, insanity is the fruit of demon possession. Today, psychologists would have diagnosed this man as schizophrenic. The real problem which this man suffered from was demons. This is why I believe very strongly that all thirty-nine people in the cult were demon possessed, simply because they were insane. No one kills themselves unless they are insane. The Bible describes insanity as demon possession.

Once the demons were cast out of this man the Bible says,

and the [town's] people went out to see what had happened. When they came to Jesus, they found the man from whom the demons had gone out, sitting at Jesus' feet, dressed and in his right mind; and they were afraid. (Luke 8:35)

The man was **in his right mind**. His cure came through deliverance from evil spirits. I've seen the same thing happen in our day.

A second fact of demons is that they know who Jesus is. You will discover among many people who are insane that they are always talking about Jesus. The reason is because the demons in them know about Jesus. However, they pervert the truth about Christ to the demonized. Thus, the demon possessed have a warped comprehension of Jesus Christ.

This is true of the Heaven's Gate cult. They talked about Jesus all the time, but they rejected giving their lives to Him. Instead, the people gave their lives to Applewhite. I get a little disturbed that people consider this cult to be Christian. People think that they were Christians because they talked about Jesus. But remember the Bible warning in Galatians 1:7-8:

...Evidently some people are throwing you into confusion and are trying to pervert the gospel of Christ. But even if we or an angel from heaven should preach a gospel other than the one we preached to you, let him be eternally condemned!

Some people mentioned Jesus, but they have in a mind another Jesus and another gospel. Although, the Heaven's Gate talked about Jesus, they did not mean the one and only begotten Son of God. Demons in them, perverted the gospel of Christ.

A third truth about demons is that they give the demoniac extraordinary strength. It took several people to restrain this man, and even then, he broke free from their control. On another case, a demoniac whipped seven Jewish exorcists (Acts 19:16). Demoniacs do not have unlimited strength, but they do have unusual power.

A fourth reality about demons is that they usually drive people to loneliness. Concerning this man, the Bible says that the demon had driven the man **into solitary places.** As in this case, demoniacs prefer to live by themselves.

This was also true of this cult. The demons in them caused this group to isolate themselves from other people. Demons do this because they don't want anyone to discover that they are possessing them.

A fifth fact about demons is that they often drive the possessed to hurt themselves. The Bible says, "Night and day among the tombs and in the hills he would cry out and cut himself with stones" (Mark 5:5). Notice that he would "cut himself with stones."

Apparently, he tried to kill himself on many occasions. Suicide is a symptom of demon possession. It is unnatural for anyone to want to die. Demons can cause people to attempt suicide.

As far as this cult was concerned, we all know the fact that they all killed themselves, the very symptom of demon possession.

A sixth fact about demons is that they sometimes use the vocal chords of the possessed to communicate. These demons spoke through this man. This is often true for today. Demons will cry, scream, and curse through individuals. They especially like to utter curses at the person who is driving them out or those who oppose their message.

The Heaven's Gate cult utter damnation at those who disagreed with them. They wrote:

The response [to our message] was extremely animated and somewhat mixed. However, the loudest voices were those expressing ridicule, hostility, or both—so quick to judge that which they could no comprehend. This was the signal to us to begin our preparations to return "home." The weeds have taken over the garden and truly disturbed its usefulness beyond repair—it is time for the civilization to be recycled—"spaded under."

Before anyone thinks that they were nice people, read their judgment they leveled against all of humanity. They declared that the world is going to be totally destroyed because the world rejected them! This sounds like people who are demon possessed.

A seventh fact about demons is that they will leave a demonic alone for awhile. The Bible says that **many times [the demon] had seized him**. Not all the time, but many times. This implies that the demon rested at times from tormenting the man. They'll do the same today. The demoniac will have temporary relief during these seasons of rest.

There was a long season of quietness during the 70's and 80' by this cult, until they returned to proclaim their false gospel during the 90's.

Oppression verses Possession

The important question to ask is how did this demoniac from Gerasenes become demon possessed? A more important question is, what led this group into demon possession and what leads some people into demon possession today?

It should be first understood that the phrase "demon possession" is a state where demons actually inhabit the mind or body of someone. In most cases, people are simply harassed or even oppressed by demons, but not actually possessed. Possession is when a demon or demons actually inhabit the person. The demon may inhabit a person for a period of time and then leave, only to come back later.

However, just because you may not be possessed does not mean that you may not be oppressed. The Bible says, "[Jesus] went about doing good, and healing all that were oppressed of the devil" (Acts 10:38, KJV). Sickness is an "oppression of the devil," although usually it is not possession.

Oppression is when the devil, through the agency of demons, harasses a person from the **outside**, perhaps placing sickness on him or by causing various trials. Possession is when the devil, through demons, torments a person from the **inside**. In the latter case, the demons actually live inside the person whom they torment.

Satan's ultimate goal is to have his demons possess people, not simply harass. The reason is because demon possession is the strongest control that the devil can ever exercise over a person.

Foot in the Door

So how did this demoniac from Gerasenes become possessed and how did this cult become demon possessed?

No one, including this demoniac, becomes possessed overnight. There are three stages which lead people into demon possession. The first level is the suggestion stage. This is when Satan first suggests lies to you. The second level is the obsession stage. This is when you constantly think about the lies. The third and final level is the possession stage. This is when the demon inhabits you. You can't help yourself anymore. Someone else will have to deliver you.

All of these stages are fought in your mind. The devil works in the mind above all arenas.

> *For though we walk [live] in the flesh, we are not carrying on our warfare according to the flesh and using mere human weapons. For the weapons of our warfare are not physical (weapons of flesh and blood), but they are mighty before God for the overthrow and destruction of strongholds, [Inasmuch as we] refute arguments and theories and reasonings and every proud and lofty thing that sets itself up*

*against the (true) knowledge of God; and we lead every
thought and purpose away captive into the obedience of
Christ, the Messiah, the Anointed One, (2 Cor. 10:3-5,
Amp)*

Satan tries to set up **strongholds**. A stronghold is a
fortress where the enemy can hide. This passage calls these
strongholds **arguments**, **theories**, and **reasonings**. These all
relate to **thoughts.** Satan hides himself in our thoughts.

The mind is the battlefield. The heavenly realm is
Satan's headquarters. Many believers try to fight Satan at his
headquarters. This is useless. The battlefield for the believer is
located in the mind. That's where the battle is fought.

God's angels will battle Satan's angels in the heavenly
realms. But we must battle Satan in the mind. If we lose the battle there, then Satan will gain a stronghold in our lives.

When you understand where the battle is fought, then
you understand what Satan uses to influence your life. He uses
theories, reasoning, arguments, and proud thoughts to gain
inroads in your life. You fight these thoughts with the Word of
God just as Christ did when the devil tempted Him.

The Bible commands, "do not give the devil a foothold"
(Ep. 4:27). A foothold is a small opening in a door.

Imagine that a salesman arrives at your door, selling
worthless goods. You tell him that you're not interested and you
try to close the door. The salesman sticks his foot in the door.
The door can't close. Why? It can't close because the salesman
has a foothold. As long as he has a foothold, he can continue to
sell you on his goods.

This is the way Satan works. He comes to you, selling his
worthless goods—temptations, sickness, poverty, trials, and
deceptions. Of course, you reject his goods on the bases of the
Word of God. You use the Word on Satan.

What does he try, then? He tries to keep a foothold by
setting up a contrary thought in your mind. He does it through
a suggestion. A **suggestion** is the first stage toward demon possession.

A suggestion is a thought which enters your mind. It
may be in the form of a theory. The thought may simply seem
reasonable, though unscriptural. The thought may even be a

fine-sounding argument against the clear teaching of the Scriptures.

Paul writes, "I tell you this so that no one may deceive you by fine-sounding arguments" (Col. 2:4). Others may present sensible arguments as to why you don't have to act on the commandments of God, or why you can't claim the promises of God. As long as you reject those thoughts, then those thoughts die unborn. They can't produce anything destructive.

There are many thoughts which come to your mind everyday. As the old saying goes, "You can't stop birds from flying in the air, but you can stop them from making a nest in your hair." You can't stop the devil from making suggestions to you, but you can stop from receiving them. If you receive them, then they become a stronghold.

Once they become a stronghold, then you have entered the second stage toward demon possession. This stage is called **obsession.**

At this stage you are obsessed with wrong thoughts. You have trouble getting them out of your mind. You constantly think about them. They begin to rule your life. If you continue to allow them to stay in your mind, then you open the door to possession.

Possession is the final stage toward total demonic control. This is a very serious stage. At this stage, you are helpless in freeing yourself from demons. You will need someone else to deliver you. There are no examples in the Bible of people expelling demons from themselves. There is no teaching about instructing disciples on how to conduct a self-deliverance session. It just doesn't happen.

So long as a person keeps from being possessed, then he has the ability to resist the devil. If you have come to this final stage, then you need a person with strong faith to help you.

Mass Murderers

For example, a mass murderer is definitely demon possessed. No one in their right mind commits multiple murders. Demons cause people to do this.

How does a mass murderer get into this condition? He did not begin this way. He may have started out to be a nice person, but something went wrong. He began to entertain a suggestion from Satan. That suggestion turned into an obsession. Eventually, the obsession opened the door to demonic possession, so that the person did things which he was not capable of stopping.

You don't simply tell a mass murderer, "Now, stop killing!" He can't stop. He's possessed. He can't help himself anymore.

His only cure is deliverance from evil spirits. Once he is delivered, then he now has control over his actions, unless he returns to his old pattern of thinking. If he returns to his old ways, then the demon will come back and bring more spirits worse than itself, so the man will even become worse than before (Matt. 12:45).

Because of this danger, I don't suggest that a mass murderer be freed from prison after he's delivered. I leave justice to the judicial system. I'm simply pointing out that a mass murderer was not born this way, but was possessed along the way. The other fact I want people to understand is that, unless demons are cast out of him, then, freeing him will only endanger the lives of others. No amount of psychological treatment will cure him unless he is delivered.

In the process of writing this chapter, I connected to the Internet to find James Dobson's interview with famed mass murderer, Ted Bundy. I found it on a server called Opendoor. I found that extremely providential. We're talking about the open door to demonic possession.

Ted Bundy started out living a normal life. There was no physical abuse or fighting in his home. The instrument which led Bundy down the destructive path was pornography. He innocently stumbled across a detective magazine. Not what you call pornography. But this magazine depicted women, dressed scantly, helplessly fighting off attackers. This led Bundy to experiment with harder stuff. This addiction finally led to possession.

As he puts it in his own words: "...You reach the jumping off point where you begin to wonder if maybe actually doing it will give you that which is beyond just reading about it or looking at it..." (Focus on the Family). Do you see what happened? He was so obsessed with pornography that he finally became possessed with it. This led him to demon possession.

Someone may object, "A lot of people read pornography and don't hurt anyone, much less become mass murderers."

I'm not saying that any one who delves into pornography will be a mass murderer. It take more than viewing pornography to make someone into a mass murderer. It takes demons to do this. I'm simply pointing out that pornography can open the door to demons. Demons may inhabit or they may not. That's their choice as well as Satan's design on each person's life.

As in Ted Bundy's case, Satan sent his most wicked spirits into his life. In your case, Satan may have to settle for sending other spirits which may not be as wicked, but will nonetheless, cause you to do evil things.

For example, spirits may cause many men watching pornography to jump from that to prostitutes. Other's simply divorce their wives for their mistresses. Still others are so obsessed with sex that they lose their spiritual zeal for the Lord. In all these cases, demons are at work in destroying their lives. Their depravation will be determined by how wicked the spirits are that are working in their lives.

The prevention of demon possession lies in nipping sinful thoughts before they can turn into obsession. If you give Satan a foot, then he will take a mile. Don't be fooled into thinking that a little obsession won't lead to possession. Many have thought the same thing, and today, they are tormented by demons. Don't let it happen to you.

And, of course, this is what happened with the Heaven's Gate cult. They began to entertain the thought of suicide. At first, they preached against the suicides of other cults. But they allowed a foothold to get control of their mind. The suggestion to kill themselves turned into an obsession, until they finally became possessed with doing it. And just like Bundy, they jumped from thinking about it to doing it.

It's a sad lesson on the power Satan tries to exercise over the mind.

Chapter 9

Brain Washed

"For my thoughts are not your thoughts,
neither are your ways my ways," declares the Lord.
—Is. 55:8

Thoughts precede actions. Every deed came forth from a thought. People often say, "I don't know what got into me to do that." They did that because a thought got into them. The thought may have been brooding for a long time, but finally the seed of thought produced a harvest of action. You might as well accept the fact that all actions are preceded by thoughts.

Quit saying, "I wonder why this cult killed themselves." They killed themselves because they were constantly thinking about it. They did what they thought to do.

Proverbs 23:7 (KJV) says, "For as he thinketh in his heart, so is he". The word "thinketh" is a continual verb. It means that a person becomes what he constantly thinks about. Proverbs 4:23 reaffirms this, "Above all else, guard your heart, for it is the well spring of life." Put in contemporary terms, "Your mind is the manufacturing center of your life. It produces your life." Jesus is even more pointed:

The good man brings good things out of the good stored
up in him, and the evil man brings evil things out of the evil
stored up in him. (Matt. 12:35)

The Mind is a Computer

Your mind is like a computer—it stores information. A computer can only perform functions according to the software that is in it. The mind is the hard drive. The software is the information your mind has received and accepted. Just as there are viruses in the computer world, there are viruses of the mind. Viruses are contracted when people copy unauthorized software.

Listen, when you receive unauthorized knowledge from people, you are copying unauthorized software and may receive viruses from them. This will cause your mind to malfunction. The only hope is to clean your mind from these diseases that others have given you. No one is authorized to impart knowledge to you. The only authorized software is *"Word Perfect—the Bible."* This will make your mind perfect.

Herff Applewhite, who was into computers, thought that he was the authorized man to impart knowledge to people. He was deceived. The Bible is the only authorized software available.

This is why God says, "My thoughts are not your thoughts." God shows us that He is the only One authorized to change your mind. He is the only One Who can brain wash you—clean your mind from filth.

God says, "Without **My** thoughts, you will continue on **your** *ways.*" We want to follow God's ways, not our own. This can only be done by receiving God's thoughts. His thoughts are in the Bible.

The Bible is God's Thoughts

No one knows the thoughts of a man, except the man himself. You cannot read minds. There is only one way to find out what a person is thinking, and that is to listen to what he says. Words reveal the thoughts of a person.

1 Corinthians 2:11 says, "...no one knows the thoughts of God except the Spirit of God." The Bible was produced when "men spoke from God as they were carried along by the Holy

Spirit" (2 Pet. 1:21). The Bible is a Spirit-produced boo
Scripture is God-breathed" (2 Tim. 3:16). God breathed o_
Bible. Have you copied on the computer of your mind this w_
derful software?

Renewed Minds Produces Transformed People

> *Do not conform any longer to the pattern of this world,*
> *but be transformed by the renewing of your mind. Then you*
> *will be able to test and approve what God's will is —his*
> *good, pleasing and perfect will. (Romans 12:2)*

One translation of this verse says, "Don't let the world
around you squeeze you into its own mold" (Phi). Squeezing
describes perfectly what the world is trying to do to you. It's trying to squeeze the life of God out of you. Don't let it.

God put His divine nature and power inside your spirit.
Your spirit is the new person created like God. Your spirit has all
the divine attributes to radically change your life. But the world
wants you to act like them—sinful, sick, defeated, and poor!

Many Christians act like the world because their minds
have never been renewed with the Word of God. Worldliness is
more than living an immoral lifestyle. It is living like the world.
The world is powerless. God wants believers to live in the power
of God.

God wants "transformed" believers. **Be transformed by
the renewing of the mind.** The word "transformed" is the same
word that is used in the "transfiguration" of Christ. The Greek
word is *metamorphoo*. It is where we get our modern word "metamorphosis."

A metamorphosis is a complete transformation, much
like a caterpillar turning into a beautiful butterfly. You can't tell
by looking at a butterfly that it once was a creepy, ugly caterpillar. This is the way it should be with us. We should not resemble
the ugly world. We are set apart. We are a "peculiar" people.
The only way to change is by renewing our minds.

We are to be "transformed into [Christ] likeness" (2
Cor. 3:18). A believer thinks he is transformed if he is a nice

moral person. Even sinners can act moral. We are called to be radically changed so that we resemble Christ in every way.

When confronted with people with diseases, Jesus stretched forth his hands and healed them. When facing a storm, He rebuked it, and the storm became calm. When demons used the vocal chords of the possessed to shout blasphemies at Christ, Jesus simply told demons to shut up and come out, and they did.

This is the way you should act. You will have to be transformed to act this way. The only way to change is to renew your mind.

I believe that the Church is partially responsible for the rise in cults in our day. Many of the people who have joined cults were once part of the Christian religion, but they did not see transformed people in the Church. Instead, they saw hypocrites. They saw the Church like a country club. It's time that we get serious, and be radically changed and be like Christ. But to do this we have to get rid of a lot of religious traditions.

Delete? Yes!

Those who work to help get people out of the cults talk about the need to deprogram those in the cults. Well, not only do those in the cults need to be deprogrammed, but so does everyone else.

The world and religion has given you a lot of wrong information about life that you need to erase. When you work on a computer and program new information, the computer will ask, "Do you want to delete?" You answer either yes or no. When you answer yes, it asks, "Are you sure?"

When you are confronted with the truth of God Word, God's Spirit will ask you about the old program that you received from the world, "Do you want to delete?" Answer, "Yes!" But the devil comes and asks, "Are you sure?" He wants you to keep the old program of the world.

What wrong information do you need to delete? Everything that does not line up with the Word of God needs to be deleted. For example, the world says, "If it feels good do it."

Yet, the Bible says, "If your right eye causes you to sin, gouge it out and throw it away. It is better for you to lose one part of your body than for your whole body to be thrown into hell" (Matt. 5:29). You need to delete the old and replace it with the new program of God's Word.

The world says, "If you're sick, take two aspirins and call the doctor." The Bible says, "I am the Lord, who heals you" (Ex. 15:26). God's Word is medicine to all your flesh (Prov. 4:22).

The world teaches, "If someone hurts you, then don't get mad—get even." However the Bible says, "Do not take revenge, my friends, but leave room for God's wrath" (Rom. 12:19). Turn the other cheek (Matt. 5:39).

The world convinces people, "If you are in financial straits, then worry." God's Word teaches different, "So do not worry, saying, 'What shall we eat?' or 'What shall we drink?' or 'What shall we wear?'…But seek first his [God's] kingdom, and his righteousness, and all these things will be given to you as well" (Matt. 6:31, 33).

The world and sometimes religion says, "You'll be saved if your good deeds out weigh your bad deeds." But God's Word says, "For it is by grace you have been saved, through faith—and this not from yourselves, it is the gift of God—not by works, so that no one can boast" (Ep. 2:8-9).

There are many other philosophies that the world has adopted which you need to delete from your hard drive—your mind!

Three Sources of Thoughts

All thoughts come from one of three sources: God, the five senses, or the devil. God's thoughts are recorded in the Bible. When you think on that book, then your thoughts come from God. This is the only sure way of knowing whether the information you have received is truthful. "Let God be true, and every man a liar" (Rom. 3:4).

The second source of thoughts come from your five senses. How do you know whether something is cold or hot, dark or bright, sweet or sour, loud or soft? You know it by your five senses. Normally, the five senses do not mislead you. Sometimes, though, the five senses get in the way of trusting God.

This is why the Bible says, "Trust in the Lord with all your heart and lean not on your own understanding" (Pro. 3:5). Your own understanding may bring fear, worry, anger, and all kinds of ungodly emotions. After all, if there is no money in the bank, it seems logical to worry.

Your senses may tell you what is **factual**, but not **truthful**. Facts can change; God's Word cannot. God's Word will read the same today as it will a thousand years from now. God's Word still says, "My God will meet all your needs according to His glorious riches in Christ Jesus" (Phil. 4:19). That's a Scripture that you can bank on.

Another example of the five senses contradicting God's Word is in the area of sickness and health. You may have a debilitating sickness, and therefore, believe that it is permanent. God's Word tells you differently. Not only does God's Word tell you that you can be healed, but from God's perspective, He does not even see you sick. He sees you well. The Bible says that you are already healed by the stripes of Jesus (1 Pet. 2:24).

You may wonder how you can believe this when your five senses tell you differently. This is faith. "We live by faith, not by sight" (2 Cor. 5:7). Sight is one of the five sense. Sight represents the senses. You cannot live by faith and go by the senses at the same time. You must choose either faith or sight. Abraham had to make this choice:

> *Without weakening in his faith, he faced the fact that his body was as good as dead—since he was about a hundred years old—and that Sarah's womb was also dead. Yet he did not waver through unbelief regarding the promise of God, but was strengthened in his faith and gave glory to God, being fully persuaded that God had power to do what he had promised. (Rom. 4:19-21)*

Notice that faith does **face the fact**. Faith does not deny the existence of facts; it only affirms the preeminence of God's Word. God's Word overrules any facts.

I like to use the word F.A.C.T. as an acronym for False

Appearance Contradicting Truth. Facts often do contradict truth. Facts relate to situations and circumstances; truth relates to God's Word. Jesus prayed, "Thy word is truth" (Jn. 17:17, KJV). God's Word is truth. It is not fact. Problems are facts. Facts can change. They change when we apply God's Truth, His Word, to the circumstances.

Knowledge based on the five senses is called by many "sense knowledge." I like that term. Many try to have faith based on sense knowledge. You can't base your faith on sense knowledge. Paul writes,

> *However, as it is written: "No eye has seen, no ear has heard, no mind has conceived what God has prepared for those who love him." —but God has revealed it to us by his Spirit. (1 Cor. 2:9-10)*

The mind that bases its knowledge on what it has seen or heard can never conceive what good things God has given to the child of God. You can only know what God has given you if the Spirit reveals it to you.

> *We have not received the spirit of the world but the Spirit who is from God, that we may understand what God has freely given us. (1 Cor. 2:12)*

This kind of knowledge is "revelation knowledge." It is knowledge that is supernaturally revealed to you by the Holy Spirit. The Spirit takes the Scriptures that He inspired and then reveals them to you. You will receive knowledge that your senses may not agree is true. But your senses cannot be trusted in spiritual matters. God's Word can be trusted!

It is important to base your spiritual life on "revelation knowledge" instead of "sense knowledge." This is especially true when it comes to understanding the devil and demons. You can't see them, so how do you know they are real? You know it by the Scriptures.

People often say, "I don't believe in the devil. I haven't seen him." Ironically, in the same breath they say, "I believe in God." Yet, they haven't seen Him! You believe in God the same way you accept the existence of the devil, and that is through revelation knowledge. This kind of knowledge is the only bases for understanding the devil and his kingdom.

Satanic Thoughts

Finally, the third source of thoughts is from Satan. The devil works on the mind. Paul warns about Satan's operations in the mind:

But I am afraid that just as Eve was deceived by the serpent's cunning, your minds may somehow be led astray from your sincere and pure devotion to Christ. (2 Cor. 11:3)

This is what happened to the Heaven's Gate cult. Many of them once had a **sincere and pure devotion to Christ** until they got caught up with this cult. Applewhite and his wife, Bonnie, began to subtly introduce teachings that focused on themselves instead of Jesus Christ. Soon, the people were worshipping them instead of Christ.

Satan works to lead your mind away from Christ and His Word. He has done this to many people who started good in their walk with God. Two biblical examples are Judas and Ananias.

The worse act recorded in the Bible is when Judas betrayed Christ. What made him do such a terrible thing? John 13:2 (KJV) tells us what caused him to do it: "the devil having now put into the heart of Judas Iscariot, Simon's son, to betray him." Betrayal began in Judas's heart and mind. The Bible says that the devil put the thought in his mind.

This is what happened to Ananias. "Then Peter said, 'Ananias, how is it that Satan has so filled your heart that you have lied to the Holy Spirit" (Acts 5:3). Ananias's lie was produced by Satan filling his heart with a lie. The thought-seed planted by Satan produced the harvest-action of lying. Peter asked, "How is it that Satan has so filled your heart?" The question is rhetorical. The answer is obvious. How has Satan filled anyone's mind? By them refusing to renew it.

Any part of the mind which is not renewed will become fertile ground for Satan to plant his satanic thoughts. Those areas are the battleground for Satan. He will fight you there. And you don't stand a chance against him, until you renew that part of your mind.

You will not be prepared to battle Satan with a mind that is not renewed. The renewed mind has a "NO TRESSPASSING" sign for Satan. He can't trespass on a renewed mind. Conversely, a mind which is not renewed becomes an open door for the devil.

The point is simple: We cannot think that we are going to free people from the cults without using the Word of God. No amount of psychological maneuvers is going to ultimately work. After all, what makes a psychologist think that he is authorized to change people's minds? He is no more authorized to educate people about spiritual matters than Applewhite was. The answer to overcoming the cults is to know the Word of God.

Chapter 10

Was Exorcism Needed?

Experts on the cults and historians are predicting an avalanche of new cults, especially as we near the end of the 20th century. Because of this, we are going to see a greater number of demon possessed in our day. It is time that we study the Word of God and practice what it teaches about exorcism.

No longer can we sweep under the carpet the Bible teaching about exorcism. Instead, it is time that we apply this neglected practice in our day. It will work, but we must do it in accord with the Word of God. Let us follow the example of our Lord Jesus Christ when it comes to exorcism.

> ...when the Sabbath came, Jesus went into the synagogue and began to teach. The people were amazed at his teaching, because he taught them as one who had authority, not as the teachers of the law. Just then a man in their synagogue who was possessed by an evil spirit cried out, "What do you want with us, Jesus of Nazareth? Have you come to destroy us? I know who you are—the Holy One of God!" "Be quiet!" said Jesus sternly, "Come out of him!" The evil spirit shook the man violently and came out of him with a shriek. The people were all so amazed that they asked each other, "What is this? A new teaching— and with authority! He even gives orders to evil spirits and they obey him." (Mark 1:21-27)

Many modern psychologists try to explain these Scriptures by saying that the people in Jesus' day did not know anything about mental disorders, so they blamed demons for people's mental sicknesses. However, it was not just the people in those days who believed in demon possession, but Jesus also believed in the reality of demon possession. If demons are not real, then Jesus, the Son of God, was deceived and wrong. Therefore, Jesus would not be sinless and couldn't be the Savior of the world.

Some so-called theologians have tried to espouse the theory that when Jesus partook of our humanity, that He also partook of the ignorance and superstition of mankind, including the superstition about demons. This theory is hard to swallow. It is one thing to say that Jesus became one with our humanity, but it is another thing to say that He partook of our errors and ignorance. Jesus is the wisdom of God (1 Cor. 1:24). He never partook of ignorance and superstition.

The truth is these psychologists are the ones ignorant about evil spirits. If they can't see them, they reason that they don't exist. The Bible never claims that spirits can be seen, but surely they can be observed through their manifestations in people's lives. As much as psychologists hate to admit, more people have been helped by praying to Jesus than by seeing them.

The Ministry of Deliverance

The ministry of deliverance must be carried out in agreement with the Scriptures. The harm which has been caused by so-called ministers of deliverance is a result of them departing from the Bible and getting into extra-biblical and, worse, unbiblical practices. The Scriptures give us several important facts about Jesus' ministry of exorcism, and if we follow it we will see positive results.

First, Jesus emphasized teaching and preaching above driving out demons. In the above Scripture, the reason Jesus came into the Synagogue was to **teach**. The Bible says that the people **were amazed at His teaching**. Today, I'm amazed at the lack of teaching among ministers of deliverance.

Some people think they are called to specialize in deliverance. Exorcism should not be anyone's specialty. Every minister should specialize in teaching the Word of God to people, and then when the need arises, they can drive out demons.

Don't go to Sister Deliverance to get set free from demons. These people seem to have revolving doors with a sign that reads: Bring your paper sack with you and prepare to vomit your demons. Don't misunderstand me, I have seen people vomit after they have been delivered, but I don't look for it.

People ask, "Why does it seem that people cough or vomit when demons come out?" Well, there is Scriptural precedent for physical manifestations. The Bible says, **"The evil spirit shook the man violently and came out of him with a shriek."** It is normal for there to be physical manifestations when spirits come out, especially physical manifestations through the mouth. Notice that this spirit came out with a **shriek.**

This is exactly what happened when Philip drove out spirits, "With shrieks, evil spirits came out of many" (Acts 8:7). A shriek is a high, pitch scream. It seems that the exit for evil spirits is through the mouth. After all, it is usually our big mouth which became the open door for demons, so it stands to reason, that the mouth is the exit as well. Coughing and vomiting are manifestations of the mouth.

In my youth, I worked at a local restaurant when one of my fellow employees confided in me. She said, "Tom, I know that you're going to think I'm crazy. But I feel that I have a demon inside of me. Nearly every night when I go to bed, this spirit begins to scare me." This girl was not a charismatic. She was not even a Christian at the time. She simply believed that evil spirits were real.

I told her that I believed her and that I would try to help her. We ended the conversation and proceeded to continue working. We closed the restaurant and started cleaning up. The Lord startled me, "Tom, if you will speak to the spirit now, the demon will go."

I walked up to this girl as she was vacuuming the carpet. I said to her, "The Lord spoke to me and told me to tell the spirit to go, and it will go."

She turned off the vacuum cleaner and said, "Then tell it to go."

I pointed my finger at her—she was about ten feet away—and said to the spirit, "In the name of Jesus, I tell you evil spirit to come out of her!"

109

The moment I said that she gasped, "Ugh!" She looked startled and exclaimed, "Something came out of my mouth. What was that?"

"That was the demon. It's gone!"

Let me repeat. This girl knew nothing of the charismatic movement. She had never seen people delivered from evil spirits. She had no past experience which could cause her to psychologically make her think that the demon should come out of her mouth. But it did. This incident is similar to the biblical examples of shrieking.

In most of the deliverance's I've been involved in, the demons come out of people with shrieks. This includes screaming, yelling, growling, snarling, and similar vocal noises. On the other hand, I don't make or encourage people to do anything. I simply tell them to be set free.

Many Demons

The second fact about Jesus ministry is that He drove out demons regularly.

> *That evening after sunset the people brought to Jesus all the sick and demon-possessed. The whole town gathered at the door, and Jesus healed many who had various diseases. He also drove out many demons, but he would not let the demons speak because they knew who he was. (Mark 1:32-34)*

Jesus **drove out many demons.** Some people get the idea that there are not many demons, and the few of them are huddled in third-world countries away from us enlightened people. A famous Christian psychiatrist, writes: "I can honestly say that I have never yet seen a single case of demon possession...I believe that there probably are some demon possessed persons in various parts of the world." [The Fakers, Danny Korem and Paul Meier, as quoted in Handbook of Today's Religions, Josh McDowell and Don Stewart, page 178.]

I'm sure this doctor desires to help people, but one has

to wonder what he has been seeing all these years. Someone may say, "But these people are helped through medications." As this physician writes, "I have had hundred of patients who came to see me because they thought they were demon possessed. Scores of them heard 'demon voices' telling them evil things to do. It was at first surprising to me that all of these had dopamine deficiencies in their brains, which were readily correctable with Thorazine or any other major tranquilizer." [Ibid.]

I wonder if Thorazine could have cured the Heaven's Gate cult? If our brother were honest, he would have to say no.

Why do some demons stop manifesting themselves when the patients take tranquilizers? They stop manifesting themselves because some of these people are so sedated that demons can't express themselves. The patient's personality is restrained as well. Medication may provide some temporary relief from the voices of demons, but the permanent answer is in the power of God.

I realize that what I'm writing will offend some people, but I'm sorry. I'm sticking with Jesus and the Bible. He is enough for all of us, if we will trust Him. We need nothing else for our complete liberation.

Religious People

A third fact about the ministry of deliverance as seen through Christ is that He drove out demons from religious people, not simply from pagans. Notice that Jesus drove out a demon from a man who was in a synagogue. Jesus was not in a Voodoo ceremony when the demon cried out to Jesus. He was in an Orthodox Jewish place of worship.

I bring this up because many Christians assume that demons could never be in church. I wish this were true, but it's not. Someone may object, "Demons can't enter Christians because they are the temple of the Holy Spirit."

It's true that our bodies are the temple of the Holy Spirit. If we keep them pure then surely no demon will enter it. The trouble is that many believers yield to fleshly sins. When they do, then they open themselves to demons.

THE HEAVEN'S GATE SUICIDE

It's interesting to note that the passage which mentions us being the temple of the Spirit was written to warn Christians from committing sexual sins.

> *Flee from sexual immorality...Do you not know that your body is a temple of the Holy Spirit...Therefore honor God with your body." (1 Cor. 6:18-20)*

This passage in no way infers that demons cannot inhabit the believer's body. On the contrary, this passage encourages believers to keep their bodies pure for the Holy Spirit so that they will not be habitations for demons. As Paul says latter in that same letter:

> *...I do not want you to be participants with demons. You cannot drink the cup of the Lord and the cup of demons too; you cannot have a part in both the Lord's table and the table of demons. Are we trying to arouse the Lord's jealousy? Are we stronger than he? (1 Cor. 10:20-21)*

This brings us to a controversy that has brooded in the body of Christ for years, and that deals with the question: Can Christians be demon possessed? I like Reinhard Bonnke's answer: "Can flies sit on a hot stove?"

Demons can not inhabit a believer who is on fire for the Lord. But they definitely can dwell with cold Christians.

This was the problem with many of the people at Rancho Santa Fe. Many of those people once were Christians, but they were not really serving the Lord passionately. They were prime targets of the enemy.

Not Everyone is Possessed

The fourth fact about exorcism is this: Jesus did not drive out demons from everyone. In the case of the demoniac in the synagogue, Jesus drove out a demon from him only. No one else was delivered. He did not hand out barf bags to everyone and say, "All right people, get ready to be delivered from demons."

112

It seems that the body of Christ can't walk down the middle of the road in this area. They either fall into a ditch on one side or the other. You hear people teach that it is impossible for Christians to be possessed or you hear another give the impression that everyone has demons. Neither is true.

Demons do inhabit many people, but not most people. For example, there is no mention about any of the apostles, except, perhaps, Judas, ever having demons. They were humans, made mistakes, did dumb things, but not once did demons ever possess them. The closest they got to demon possession was when Peter rebuked Christ. Jesus said to him, "Get behind me, Satan! (Matt. 16:23). However, Jesus did not drive out demons from Peter.

Don't Talk with Demons

A fifth fact about Jesus and demons is this: He did not usually hold conversations with demons. He said, **"Be quiet! Come out of him!"**

It is true that on one occasion Jesus asked a demon his name, but this was because the demon refused to go. You may ask a demon its name if they refuse to depart, but it's not wise to hold a conversation with it. Ordinarily, Jesus shut the mouths of demons. This is the normal way of deliverance.

My Personal Experience

I heard someone pound on my door. As I opened it, one of my members barged through, "Tom, you have to come with me quickly! There's a man who's demon possessed. I and some others need your help to drive out the demons!" I went with him.

As I arrived, there were about four men who were trying to excise the demons from this man. Everyone was shouting different things, "What's your name!" "Tell us about the realm of the spirit." "Where did you come from?" "Recount to us about the role of demons in Mexico." Everyone was more interested in talking with the demons than casting them out.

The people would grab the man and try to hold him

down. But the demoniac simply threw them across the room.

One guy turned to me, "Tom, these demons don't want to leave. We've been at it for several hours. Why don't you give it a try. Maybe you can cast them out."

I walked over to this man, reached out my right hand and touched his shoulder. Looking him in the eyes, I said, "I'm not talking to the demons, I'm talking to you, sir. Please come over here to the couch and sit down with me." He did.

I asked him, "How long have you been like this?"

"For many years, I have heard these demons talk to me and speak through me. I want to be free, but I can't."

"Yes you can!" I assured him. "And I believe that you will be set free today."

"Can you drive out the demons from me?"

"I sure can with God's power."

He grinned, "I think you can."

"I know I can." I laid my hands on the man and said calmly, yet sternly, "In the name of Jesus, I command all the evil spirits to come out of him." I named several which I believed were in him.

No sooner had I said this, the man looked up at me and smiled wide, "They're gone!" The other men all sensed that the spirits had left him.

That night, the leader of this group came to me privately and asked, "Tom, what were we doing wrong? Why couldn't we drive out the spirits?"

I explained to him, "You should not hold conversations with demons. By doing that, you prolong the deliverance. Simply, take your authority over the spirits and cast them out!" He accepted what I said.

Give Orders to Demons

This brings us to the six principle about exorcism as witnessed in the ministry of Jesus, and that is this: Jesus drove out demons with His word.

When Jesus drove out the demon from the man in the synagogue, the people were astonished on how He drove out the demon. They said, "**He even gives orders to evil spirits and they obey him.**" They weren't used to any one driving out demons with simply their words. This is the way Jesus delivered people from demons. Another Scripture says,

> *When evening came, many who were demon-possessed were brought to [Jesus], and he drove out the spirits with a word and healed all the sick. (Matt. 8:16)*

Jesus expelled demons with simply His word. He used nothing else.

I'm surprised how many Christians depend on various methods of casting out demons. The only method you need is your words. Your words can drive out demons.

Yet, when people try to perform an exorcism, they bring out the holy water, a crucifix, candles, incense, prayer beads, a blessed Bible, a prayer book, and anything else they think will be effective to drive out the demons. But they lack one thing: faith.

Listen, if you want to be successful at driving out demons, then take all your religious paraphernalia, including the latest deliverance book with all the new techniques of exorcism and find the nearest garbage can and dump all the unnecessary accessories in it. Then you'll be ready to drive out demons.

Perverting Exorcism

The Bible records one instance of the disciples failing to drive out a demon. When Jesus arrived and saw the boy still possessed, Jesus rebuked the disciples and said, "O unbelieving and perverse generation" (Matt. 17:17). Jesus not only called them unbelieving, He also called them "perverse."

The word perverse means to be willfully determined not to do what is expected or desired. Instead, it is to do the contrary. All Christ expected of His disciples was for them to use His name to drive out demons. Evidently, the disciples must have resorted to other means of driving out the demon for

Christ to call them perverse. They probably resorted to the old Jewish methods of exorcism.

The Jewish procedure of exorcism was very elaborate. It contained all kinds of rituals and ceremonies, much like the traditional ceremony of exorcism practiced today by many religions.

Unfortunately many Christians resort to other means of driving out demons, other than the one means which Christ told us to depend on—and that's His name.

Don't depend on anything except the name of Jesus. That name has the authority to make demons bow. With the power of the Holy Spirit and your knowledge of the Word of God, you are fully equipped to drive out demons.

Chapter 11

How to Free People From Deception

Is there is anything that we as Christians can do to free people from the cults? Most assuredly, yes! We are not helpless. We have a power that is far greater than any cult. We have the power of the Holy Spirit in us. As the Bible says, "the one who is in you is greater than the one who is in the world" (1 Jn. 4:4).

Sometimes we feel helpless, but we truly are not. We can exercise the power of prayer to free people from the cults. But it won't be wimpy prayer that will free them. It will take warfare prayer to do it.

The most important lesson I want to share with you in this book is to teach you how to free someone from the deception of cults. It doesn't matter what kind of cult they are in, there is a way to set people free. What I am going to share with you will also empower you to help ordinary people get saved, even if they are not in cults.

You may have loved ones who are not in cults but you would like to see them get saved anyway. Let's face it, whether someone is in a cult or a member in good standing with society, he is still lost and will be doomed to eternal judgment if he does not get saved. I suppose the danger in focusing on cults is the misconception that only people in cults need Christ. But the truth is, everyone needs Christ: from the President to the janitor.

You see, someone does not have to be in a cult to be lost; he can be an ordinary person and be the best citizen—and still be lost.

How God Taught Me to Save the Lost

God taught me how to save the lost many years ago when I lived with my grandfather.

My grandfather was an atheist, not a sophisticated one, but one nevertheless. I would tell him everything I knew about God and Jesus, which wasn't much at the time, but I shared it with him in sincerity.

He argued back, "I don't believe there is a God in heaven. You see this chair, this is god. And this table, it's god, too. This world is the only god I know."

I pleaded with him, "Grandpa, you're wrong. There is a God in heaven, and He loved you so much that He sent His only begotten Son, Jesus Christ, to save you so that you can have eternal life with God in heaven."

"I don't believe in Jesus Christ. He was just a man like us."

Those words crushed me. I couldn't understand how my grandpa could be so wrong and not see who Jesus really is. He would frustrate me.

One day, I was praying to God that He would save my grandpa. As I was praying, the Lord spoke to me, "Tom, you keep asking Me to save your grandpa, as if you needed to talk Me into it. I want him to get saved. The problem is not with Me. I'm not willing that any should perish (2 Pet. 3:9). The trouble is with the devil."

From that point, the Lord taught me about the role Satan plays in keeping people from being converted. He first took me to the passage in 2 Corinthians 4:4:

The god of this age has blinded the minds of unbelievers, so that they cannot see the light of the gospel of the glory of Christ...(2 Cor. 4:4)

The Lord explained to me, "I'm not the god of this age, Satan is. Satan is the god of all unbelievers. It doesn't do much good to ask Me to save unbelievers, because I'm not their personal god. Yes, I'm the God of all mankind, but I'm not their personal Lord and Savior (Rom. 10:9-10). Now, you can ask Me to send forth laborers into the harvest field (Matt. 9:38). The laborers are My children. I can tell them what to do. But it's not correct for Me to order unbelievers to get saved. What good would it do for Me to order unbelievers to get saved, if no one was witnessing to them? Ask Me, instead, to send people across their path so they can hear the Gospel."

So I asked God to send people to my grandpa. When I did, the Lord said, "Now, I'm sending you to your grandfather. You're the laborer to him."

Then the Lord said something to me which I will never forget, "Remember this: you are the answer to many people's prayers." I realized that He was showing me that many others were praying for their unsaved loved ones, and that God was sending me as a laborer to reap their unsaved loved ones.

Concerning my grandfather, I said, "But Lord, I have been witnessing to him; he doesn't seem to respond."

The Lord explained the reason, "Your grandfather, if he understood the gospel, would love to get saved. The trouble is that the god of this age has blinded his mind from comprehending the gospel."

"What do I do then?"

"I have given you My authority and power to bind the devil from blinding your grandpa's mind. Say out loud to him, 'I bind you devil from blinding my grandpa's mind! I tell you to stop it, now, in Jesus name!'"

"Are you telling me that the only reason why my grandpa hasn't gotten saved was because the devil has blinded his mind?"

"Yes."

"You must give me another Scripture to prove this."

The Lord took me to the parable of the sower. He made me study the people along the path who heard the Word:

> *Those along the path are the ones who hear, and then the devil comes and takes away the word from their hearts, so that they may not believe and be saved. (Luke 8:12)*

The Lord asked me, "Why did those people along the path not believe and get saved?"

I looked carefully, and then I saw it, "I see Lord, the Bible says that the **devil comes and takes away the word from their hearts**. The reason why they did not believe was because the devil stole the Word from them."

"That's right! You see, many of My people think that unbelievers don't get saved because they choose not to get saved. The truth is, many unbelievers would choose to get saved if the devil did not steal the Word from their hearts. So stop the devil from stealing the Word by binding him. Bind him with your words! Tell him to stop! He'll have to obey you."

Listen to me carefully: I don't care what you have heard, none of the Heaven's Gate cult chose to kill themselves. They were deceived into doing it. Pure and simple.

After the Lord explained this passage, He then showed me one more passage related to this. It was the passage in Acts 26:16-18. This is when Jesus appointed Paul as a preacher:

> *"Now get up and stand on your feet. I have appeared to you to appoint you as a servant and as a witness of what you have seen of me and what I will show you. I will rescue you from your own people and from the Gentiles. I am sending you to them to open their eyes and turn them from darkness to light, and from the power of Satan to God, so that they may receive forgiveness of sins and a place among those who are sanctified by faith in me."*

I saw it again. Paul was not called to plead with God for the salvation of the lost. Paul was called to personally exercise his God-given authority to **open their eyes and turn them from darkness to light, and from the power of Satan to God.** The result would be the salvation of the lost.

We, too, have that same authority! We turn people from the power of Satan through preaching the gospel to them and by binding the devil.

Once the Lord showed me this last passage, I walked into my grandfather's bedroom and said, "Grandpa, I realize that you want to get saved if you understood the Gospel. The devil is the one who is blinding your mind, so I'm going to bind him from your life, right now."

There in his bedroom, I shouted at the devil and told

him to leave my grandpa. My grandpa just stood there, speech-less. I left the room, confident that my grandpa would get saved.

Before long, I married my wife, Sonia. A few months after our marriage, the Lord led my wife and me to pray the prayer of agreement according to Matthew 18:19 for my grand-father to get saved. "Again, I tell you that if two of you on earth agree about anything you ask for, it will be done for you by my Father in heaven."

It was a Monday morning, and I was going to visit him as usual. I told Sonia, "The Lord shows me that today my grandfa-ther is going to get saved. So, please, join me in prayer that it will happen as God shows me." We prayed and agreed that my visit with Grandpa would result in his salvation.

I drove to his house and walked into his bedroom with a big smile on my face. My grandfather was laying in bed sick. I knelt beside his bed and said, "Grandpa, the Lord shows me that you're ready to get saved. Are you ready to get saved?"

Without hesitation, he nodded, "I'm ready." I led him into the sinner's prayer. We wept as we prayed together.

Soon after this, my wife and I started our first church. Although my grandpa was incapacitated through old age, he asked my dad to take him to my new church.

I'll never forget it. My dad practically carried him to church and sat him down on a chair in the rear.

As everyone stood up to sing to the Lord, my grandpa made the biggest effort to stand up, and he did. With his left hand holding a chair in front of him for balance, he lifted his other hand to praise the Lord along with the rest of us.

That was the first and last service which he was able to attend. His health continued to deteriorate until he died soon after attending our church. Now, my grandfather is in heaven, the real place full of happiness and joy!

A Prayer That Works

If my prayer can work for an atheist, it can work for a cult member as well. Pray this prayer for the person you desire to get saved. This prayer is simple, but powerful. Pray:

Father, in the name of Jesus, my prayer and heart's desire is for _____ to be saved. According to your Word, You are not willing that any person should perish, but that all should come to repentance. I ask You, Father, to send forth laborers who will witness to _____. Open _____ eyes that he/she may see the glorious gospel of Jesus Christ. I now take my authority as a child of God, and I bind the devil, who is the god of this world, from blinding his/her mind. I command you to stop deceiving _____! Satan, you will not steal the Word of God which is planted into _____ heart. I break your power over his/her life right now! _____ is now set free from Satan's power. I turn _____ from darkness to light, from the power of Satan to the power of God. _____ now will get saved, and receive forgiveness of sins and a place among those who are sanctified. In Jesus Name, I declare it so! Amen.

A Prayer for Salvation

Perhaps you read this book more out of curiosity about the Heaven's Gate cult, and now you realize that you need salvation. It is never too late to change. If my grandfather could give his life to Christ at the age of eighty-two, then surely you can as well. Repeat the following prayer out loud and mean it. As you pray it, God will save you:

Dear God in Heaven, I come to you in the name of Jesus Christ. I repent of my sins and ask you to forgive me. I accept your forgiveness. I believe that Jesus rose from the dead and is alive. I make Jesus the Lord of my life. Lord Jesus, come into my heart right now. According to God's Word, I am saved.

Amen!

If you prayed this prayer, then let me hear from you. And when you write feel free to enclose your prayer requests, letters, questions, or comments.

Tom Brown
P.O. Box 27275
El Paso, TX 79926
email: tombrown@whc.net

THE HEAVEN'S GATE SUICIDE

About the Author

Tom Brown is the founder and pastor of two growing congregations in El Paso, Texas, Word of Life Church and River of Life Church. Among his duties as pastor, he finds time to publish his city's largest and longest running Christian publication called *Good News El Paso.* He and his wife, Sonia, hosts a weekly television program by the same name. Along with his contributions in writing for his local paper, he writes for the larger body of Christ; his book, *You Can Predict Your Future,* has blessed many. He is also president of the Charismatic Bible School which is equipping believers for full-time ministry. He has the rare combination of being a gifted speaker and writer as well as one who moves mightily in the gifts of the Spirit. With all of his accomplishments, Tom is most committed to his wife Sonia and three children: Justin, Faith, and Caleb. They live together in El Paso. You can visit Tom on the Internet at www.tbm.org.

Other Materials by Tom Brown

You Can Predict Your Future
192 page book $6.99

You'll learn how to discern God's will for your life so that you can boldly speak His Word out of your mouth in order to predict your future. This is one of the great inspirational books of our time. It's destined to become a classic!

You Can Predict Your Future
4 Tape Album $19.99

This dynamic series will encourage you to keep your tongue from speaking anything which is contrary to God's Word. It will answer many questions about faith and positive confession.

The Heaven's Gate Suicide:
Unlocking the answer to why it happened
4 Tape Album $19.99

Demons caused these people to kill themselves. Remarkable yet true. Tom investigates the role demons played in the suicide, and he explores how demons work today. These tapes could save your life and the life of the people you love.

Postage and handling are included in the prices.

Place your order by making checks or money orders (U.S. funds only) payable to:

Tom Brown Ministries
P.O. Box 27275
El Paso, TX 79926
855-9673

Schedule a Seminar

If you would like to schedule a seminar on the subject of the Heaven's Gate Suicide, then contact the author soon while this topic is hot, and expect huge crowds to come. Contact the author by letter, phone, or email:

Tom Brown
P. O. Box 27275
El Paso, TX 79926
(915) 857- 0962
tombrown@whc.net

Visit
Tom Brown Ministries

Over the Internet
at WWW.TBM.ORG

Read Inspiring Articles
Discover Tom's Favorite Internet Links
Share in the chat room
Ask Tom Bible Questions
Look up your favorite Spirit-filled church or ministry

The home page may be under construction, so all services may not be provided.